BASKETBALL

ITS ORIGIN AND DEVELOPMENT

BY

JAMES NAISMITH

INVENTOR OF THE GAME

Introduction to the Bison Books Edition
by William J. Baker

University of Nebraska Press
Lincoln and London

⊗ The paper in this book meets the minimum requirements
of American National Standard for Information Sciences—
Permanence of Paper for Printed Library Materials,
ANSI Z39.48-1984.

First Bison Books printing: 1996
Most recent printing indicated by the last digit below:
10   9   8   7   6   5   4   3   2

Library of Congress Cataloging-in-Publication Data
Naismith, James, 1861–1939.
Basketball: its origin and development / by James Naismith,
inventor of the game; introduction to the Bison books edition
by William J. Baker.
p.   cm.
Originally published: New York: Association Press, 1941.
Includes index.
ISBN 0-8032-8370-9 (alk. paper)
1. Basketball—History.   I. Title.
GV885.N35   1996
796.323—dc20
95-44893   CIP

Reprinted from the original 1941 edition by Association Press,
New York. This Bison Books edition follows the original in
beginning chapter 1 on arabic page 13.

INTRODUCTION

William J. Baker

James Naismith's *Basketball: Its Origins and Development*
first appeared in print in 1941 under the auspices of the
Young Men's Christian Association (YMCA), in celebration
of the birth of basketball fifty years earlier. Unfortunately,
1941 was a bad year for birthday parties. As Nazi Ger-
many intensified its air attack and tightened a sea block-
ade of Britain, destructive forces stalked the earth. Boast-
ing quick victories in Yugoslavia, Greece, and Crete,
German troops invaded the Soviet Union and General
Edwin Rommel's Africa Corps assaulted Libya. All the
while, German submarines engaged in a search-and-de-
stroy mission against supplies being shipped from North
America. Finally, the United States officially entered the
war after a surprise Japanese attack on Pearl Harbor. That
"day of infamy" occurred on 7 December 1941, within the
same month that James Naismith created basketball half
a century earlier. The pressures of war snuffed out all the
birthday candles.

That was a double pity, for in normal times basketball
enthusiasts would have had much to celebrate. Their game
had grown from a simple YMCA activity to a highly competitive sport sponsored by thousands of colleges, high
schools, churches and industries. Between the two world
wars, innumerable small midwestern towns took to basketball as a badge of local pride. Several highly visible

professional teams toured the country; college attendance figures steadily grew. By 1941, New York's Madison Square Garden was regularly filled for college basketball doubleheaders and tournaments.

Building on foundations laid in the mid-thirties, promoter Ned Irish in 1938 led in the creation of the National Invitational Tournament (NIT). Four teams from the New York City area and two nationally recognized squads attracted more than 16,000 spectators for the finals at Madison Square Garden. The NIT's success stirred college coaches to create a season-end play-off scheme more directly under their control, and in 1939 the National Collegiate Athletic Association (NCAA) tournament was quietly born at Northwestern University. Scant publicity kept the attendance low, causing that first NCAA tournament to lose money. Yet the two premier college basketball tournaments were in place prior to the war, ready to capitalize on a postwar boom.

Basketball also enjoyed dramatic international expansion in the 1930s. As Naismith explains in chapter 8, the infant game was first spread around the world by believers in the YMCA gospel of godliness and good games. Not until 1932, however, was an international gathering devoted specifically to basketball. Out of that Geneva conference came the International Federation of Amateur Basketball (IFBA). Four years later, at Berlin, the hoop game received the ultimate international recognition when it took its place on the quadrennial Olympic program.

Naismith's book resonates with this widespread popularity of basketball. He describes it in great detail; he offers various explanations for it. Most of all, he assumes the global appeal of a game that he fashioned with his own hands. His self-appointed task was to explain how and why the game was born, and the manner of its subsequent development.

The idea for the book originated some five or six years prior to publication, when the family nudged the aged Naismith to put his story on paper. In his mid-seventies, he was retired in Lawrence after four decades of teaching physical education at the University of Kansas. He remained physically active and verbally gifted, but he was literarily disinclined. His spelling and grammar were poor; problems of focus and sequence made the process of writing a miserably slow ordeal. For well over a year he struggled unsuccessfully to give orderly expression to his memories. Finally his eldest son, Jack, joined him for a summer at a family cabin on the Kaw River, near Lawrence, taking dictation while Naismith read from scattered essays and notes.

The father's tendency to ramble, to repeat himself, and to trail off in vague references drove the son to distraction. Remembering an English professor who had helped him with his own prose during his university days, Jack turned to her for help. For $150 she put the manuscript through several drafts. She corrected spelling and grammar errors, pruned repetitious passages, and tightened up the narrative. Like the game of basketball itself, Naismith's *Basketball* is a carefully crafted piece of art. The prose does not soar, but it is clear and coherent, disarmingly simple and direct.

Portions of it were lifted directly from Naismith's previously published essays. Shortly after creating the game, he briefly described "Basket Ball" and its thirteen original rules for a YMCA journal, *The Triangle* (15 January 1892). In 1914 he embellished his story at the eighth annual convention of the National Collegiate Athletic Association, published it in the *American Physical Education Review* (May 1914), then saw it reprinted as a YMCA pamphlet under the title "History and Development of Basketball." In one of the Wingate Memorial Lectures of 1931–32, he further explained to a New York City audience "How Basketball Started and Why It Grew." That lecture became a chapter in *Aims and Methods in School Athletics* (1932), edited by E. Dana Caulkins.

Beyond the various literary and personal elements that went into making Naismith's *Basketball,* the various assumptions and cultural attitudes that contributed to the making of "Naismith's new game" require some attention. New views on matters of health, religion, and competitive sport all fed into the moment when two peachbaskets first made their appearance in December 1891 on the balcony railing of that little Springfield gym.

As cities grew like mushrooms in nineteenth-century Britain and North America, health became an issue of paramount concern. Rampant urban growth produced massive problems of food and water supply, waste disposal, and congested housing. Outbreaks of contagious cholera, tuberculosis, and pneumonia periodically wiped out entire city neighborhoods. People scarcely knew the scientific causes of these maladies, nor did they have any prescriptive drugs. How, then, could one take advantage of the employment and entertainment opportunities provided by city life, yet avoid the health disasters that seemed to lurk on every street corner?

Health reformers prescribed cleanliness, proper diet, and vigorous exercise. Soap, lye, and bleach became best-selling commodities; so did faddish new health foods such as W. G. Kellogg's "corn flakes." Most of all, an exercise industry thrived in nineteenth-century cities. Mayors and city councilors worked with various private organizations to provide exercise facilities in parks, playgrounds, and gymnasiums. One of those organizations, the Young Men's Christian Association, began in London as an evangelical body of young men primarily fearful of the *moral* dangers of city life. Shortly after the YMCA came to North America in the 1850s, it began attending to the physical as well as moral needs of its members. Exercise programs and physical education lessons quickly became staple items on the YMCA menu. Without that emphasis, James Naismith would have lacked the motivation to create his new game. Not by coincidence, he earned a medical degree as well as a diploma in physical education.

In the 1880s, between his McGill B.A. and his Springfield diploma, Naismith also did a three-year stint of theological study at a Presbyterian seminary affiliated with McGill. Ordained in 1916 in order to serve as a wartime chaplain, he was well equipped to join those liberal Protestant ministers who marched at the front of the health crusade. They thought illness an evil to be combatted, a demon to be defeated. "Next to Satan and Beelzebub, the two great enemies of mankind are dyspepsia and the headache. Keep clear of them!" warned a Methodist minister to a Brooklyn congregation. It seemed "as truly a man's moral duty," announced another pastor, "to have a good digestion, and sweet breath, and strong arms, and stalwart legs, and an erect bearing as it is to read his Bible, or say his prayers, or love his neighbor as himself."

This preoccupation with health lay behind the movement of "muscular Christianity" that propelled James Naismith to invent basketball. The term was coined as a derisory reference to the robust perspective of an English cleric and novelist, Charles Kingsley, who bullishly walked and rowed great distances for his health. As a prototypical sporting parson, Kingsley provoked Victorian author and editor Leslie Stephen to dismiss muscular Christianity as an impulse to "fear God and walk a thousand miles in a thousand hours."

Kingsley's friend, Thomas Hughes, linked the health mania to competitive games in a best-selling novel, *Tom Brown's Schooldays* (1857). For all its physical roughness and potential for injury, football at Rugby School presumably improved both the moral and physical health of Tom Brown and his friends. "Muscular Christianity is Christianity applied to the treatment and use of our bodies," insisted an American admirer of Tom Brown. "It is an enforcement of the laws of health by the solemn sanctions of the New Testament."

Muscular Christianity also embodied a departure from the solemn sanctions and prohibitions of Puritan forebears. By no means were all Puritans spoilsports about all recreations, but they did think it virtuous to work hard, to avoid idle pleasures, and to abhor all activities that tended to desecrate the sabbath. By implication, if not explicit prohibition, most sports and popular pastimes were to be avoided. America's muscular Christian reaction against these puritanical attitudes significantly began in New England where the Puritan mindset remained strongest.

A Unitarian minister, Thomas Wentworth Higginson, forged the way. In nine essays for a new periodical, *The Atlantic Monthly* (1858–62), he hung the tricolor of health, religion, and athletics high for all to see. The first essay, "Saints, and Their Bodies," especially brought "physical vigor and spiritual sanctity" together in a cohesive unit. Higginson aggressively rejected the view that athleticism was in any sense detrimental to the sanctity required to devout Christians. Thus did a liberal, urbane Unitarian from Boston initiate a new way of thinking about the compatibility of religion and sport that would allow James Naismith, a more conventional Presbyterian from rural Canada, to compete athletically and even to pursue a career in physical education.

An older sister, enthralled at the prospect of young Jim becoming a clergyman, stubbornly refused to give her blessings to his athletic aspirations. Where she failed, other women succeeded in ruling the religious roost, it seems. As Ann Douglas, Barbara Welter, and Mary Ryan suggest, religion in the nineteenth century became more "feminized" than usual. Although male hierarchies of ministers, deacons, and elders remained intact, women increasingly played key roles in the day-to-day life of Protestant churches. Women far outnumbered men in church attendance and revivals, and outworked them in Sunday schools, church visitations, and missionary societies.

Nor was the church an isolated segment of nineteenth-century life. Built on the cornerstone of religion, a broad swath of middle-class culture—the home, education, and voluntary societies, for starters—came under the woman's touch, and altered accordingly. Childrearing, for example, became less patriarchal, more maternally affectionate and nourishing; tutelage in the home and school emphasized more instructional patience and emotional support than rigid discipline.

Arguably, muscular Christianity represented a reaction against these feminizing tendencies. At the least, Protestant sportsmen sought to dispel the notion that a weak and timid Jesus attracted only women and effeminate men. More broadly, muscular Christianity defined manliness in physically active, competitive terms that were familiar to male youths deprived of the simple gender verities enjoyed by their forebears. Ringing in the ears of many a muscular Christian were admonitions like the one pronounced by James Naismith's grandfather, a Scottish immigrant and hardworking carpenter in rural Ontario. "Don't think you can't master it!" he declared when young Jim struggled to help at a task. "Do it and make a man of yourself."

To Naismith's grandfather, who came of age in the early nineteenth century, a "real man" was a self-reliant, self-assertive individual who conquered the frontier or mastered a profession. Those simple beliefs withered amidst the complexities of urban life, and during the last quarter of the century another kind of male dominance, athletic prowess, became a central feature in the definition of manliness. In NorthAmerica, much more than in Britain, the YMCA played a crucial role in that transformation.

By the time Naismith arrived at Springfield in 1890, the YMCA sponsored competitive athletics in addition to its earlier commitments to evangelical piety and exercise gymnastics. Much of the credit goes to the director of the training college, Luther Halsey Gulick, whom Naismith held in highest respect. A son of missionary parents in Hawaii, Gulick attended Oberlin College and the Sargent School of Physical Training in Cambridge, Massachusetts, and came of age when professional baseball, college football, and a host of individual sports were taking organized shape. No great athlete himself, he firmly believed in a "play instinct" that needed to be stimulated and honed by competition. He also knew the popular appeal of sport for American youths, so he urged the YMCA to sweeten its religion and health offerings with sport.

Gulick first campaigned for athletics through the prime YMCA journals of the day, *The Watchman* and *Young Men's Era*. For years after its inception in 1874, *The Watchman* gave little attention to gymnasium activities and even less to competitive athletics. Gulick turned that pattern on its head when he became editor of the paper's new "Physical Department" section in 1889, and all the more for *The Watchman*'s successor, *Young Men's Era*. In addition to gymnastic news for YMCAs all around the country, Gulick reported on rowing contests, track meets, baseball games, and tennis matches sponsored by local YMCAs from Maine to California. Reportage constituted a kind of advertisement for YMCA-sponsored sport.

Strange as it might now seem, many local branches of the YMCA fielded football teams in the late nineteenth century. Before equipment, facilities, coaches, and insurance became prohibitively expensive, YMCA squads competed with each other and also against teams sponsored by athletic clubs, colleges, prep schools, and seminaries. A chorus of enthusiasts extolled the exertion of lungs, loins, and limbs required by football. Other contributors to *Young Men's Era* debated the "brutishness" of the game, but in 1890—the very autumn that James Naismith enrolled at Springfield—a team took the field representing the little YMCA training college.

Having played lacrosse and rugby at McGill University, Naismith quickly learned the rudiments of American football. He was ably assisted in that effort by the captain and coach of the Springfield team, Amos Alonzo Stagg, a star fullback on the Yale squad that in 1888 outscored its opponents 698–0. For all their Canadian and American differences, the Gillie and the Yalie were remarkably similar young men. Physically, both were short and stocky like most of their Springfield teammates; sportswriters gave the team the nickname "Stubby Christians." Religiously, both men came from Presbyterian families of firm belief and stern ethical principles. Vocationally, both had turned from theological study to YMCA work. Naismith pondered the possibility "that there might be other effective ways of doing good besides preaching"; Stagg felt "specially called to preach" but decided to do it in athletics rather than from a pulpit.

With Naismith at center and Stagg at fullback, Springfield won five of its eight games in 1890. They finished the season with a hard-fought loss, 16–10, to the perennial national champion and Stagg's alma mater, Yale. In the autumn of 1891, the Springfield team won only five games while losing eight and tying one, but consoled themselves in battles well fought against the eastern powers of the day.

Amid that excitement, Naismith was working on Luther Gulick's summer seminar assignment to create "some new game" that would take up in the winter where football left off in late fall. Years later Naismith spoke from personal experience when he recalled youths of his generation wanting the "pleasure and thrill" of athletic competition rather than physically beneficial but boring gymnastics and exercise programs. Predictably, football was the first game he attempted to modify for indoor use. He also toyed with reconfigurations of lacrosse, rugby, soccer, hockey, and baseball, but his failure to adapt any outdoor team game to the hard floor and restricted space of the gym forced Naismith to dream and scheme his way to the new game of basketball.

Except for his memories of the "duck on the pond" game of his Ontario youth, Naismith worked without any models featuring a ball tossed into a basket set above the players' heads. Various conjectures depict him getting his idea from the European outdoor game of netball. Others contend that he borrowed from an old Native American practice of throwing a ball against a backboard made of saplings, nailed halfway up a tree. Most fanciful of all is the suggestion that basketball derived from an ancient, fiercely-contested Mayan and Aztec ritualistic game in the stone ballcourts of Central America. Naismith knew about none of these games, it seems. Rather than discovered and imported from afar, basketball came into existence at a Y-junction where athletic experience linked up with a shrewd intelligence and a lively imagination.

Within four years of the game's invention, Naismith left Springfield for medical school in Denver, Colorado. To pay his way, he directed gymnastic classes and refereed basketball games at the Denver YMCA. In 1898, the medical degree finished, he took a curiously diverse assignment to manage the athletic program, serve as college chaplain, head the physical education department, and informally coach basketball at the University of Kansas. His old friend and Springfield teammate, Amos Alonzo Stagg, already a successful football coach at the University of Chicago, recommended Naismith as the "inventor of basket-ball, medical doctor, Presbyterian minister, tee-totaler, all-around athlete, non-smoker, and owner of vocabulary without cuss words."

Over the course of the next three decades, as the University of Kansas modernized in the direction of more professional specialization, Naismith's strength as a jack-of-all-trades worked to his detriment. His role as university chaplain was the first to go. Compulsory daily chapel gave way to a weekly requirement, then to voluntary student attendance at more secular lectures. Beginning with the basketball coach's slot in 1909, Naismith relinquished all of his other administrative positions to the hard-driving ambitions of young Forest "Phog" Allen. In 1919 Allen became Director of Athletics, and in 1926 he replaced Naismith as chair of the Department of Physical Education.

Glimmers of these personal setbacks scarcely appear in Naismith's recollections. Nor does he mention his domestic difficulties. When his young wife was pregnant with the second of their five children, she contracted pneumonia and typhoid fever that left her permanently deaf. For the remaining forty years of her life, she provided companionship but largely refused to participate in social gatherings. Except for the rare occasions when he was accompanied by a child, Naismith went to public events alone, or not at all.

Naismith found refuge in his physical education classes, in health and exercise research, and in weekend jaunts to pulpits within driving distance of Lawrence. He also kept up with basketball as best he could from the sidelines. He regularly attended University of Kansas games, and in 1936 Phog Allen arranged an invitation and helped raise the funds for Naismith to travel to Europe as an honored guest at the Berlin Olympics, where basketball first made its appearance as an official Olympic sport. The gods favored the Canadian-born Naismith, now a naturalized American citizen, with a gold-medal match-up between Canada and the United States. The Americans won by the modest score of 19–8.

Those Berlin games were played outdoors, often as not in a downpour of rain. Ironically, it made the games much more like the defensive, passing, and low-scoring style of basketball that Naismith created almost half a century earlier. In truth, by the time of Naismith's death in 1939, the game had passed him by. As an active and then honorary member of the national rules committee, he adamantly resisted several important rule changes. The requirement that the offensive team must get the ball past center court within ten seconds, for example, struck Naismith as a measure that pandered to the modern craze for high-scoring games. For similar reasons, and with similar ineffectiveness, in the mid-1930s he opposed the abolition of the center jump ball after each basket.

Naismith was especially out of touch in his persistent belief that his creation should be played for fun, exercise, and the building of character, not for its money-making potential. He hardly made a cent from the game he devised. Although basketball is the only major sport that has been instantaneously created, Naismith never patented his invention. Fearful of coaching too much, he refrained from selling himself primarily as a coach, nor did he ever use his reputation to endorse a product.

The final chapter of this book, "The Values of Basketball," reveals the moral core of the creator's heart. Whatever its later commercial developments, basketball was made for principled play, not for profit. This new edition of *Basketball* serves to remind us that James Naismith designed his new game for athletes to enjoy, not for coaches, television networks, or corporate sponsors to control.

PREFACE

IN WRITING of the origin and development of basketball, forty-three years after its invention, I have given little space to technical aspects of the game; but rather I have written the book in an attempt to answer a number of questions.

Since it was impossible for me to gather the data myself, I have been forced to call on men from all parts of the world for some of the information that I have used. I have mentioned some of these men in the text of the book; but they are only a few of the persons who have contributed. To the men who have used basketball and in that using have helped to develop and spread the game in the interest of sportsmanship and for the benefit of the young people of the world, I wish to express my sincere appreciation.

JAMES NAISMITH

CONTENTS

CHAPTER I

BENNIE'S CORNERS

IT WAS evening, and a group of boys had gathered at Bennie's Corners, in the northern part of Ontario, Canada. Their work was finished, and they were spending their leisure time in different kinds of contests. It was a common event, this gathering, and little did any of them realize that some of their activities would some day play an important part in the origin of the game of basketball.

Bennie's Corners was a gathering place for a group of the country boys who lived in that vicinity. At the Corners there were a blacksmith shop, a schoolhouse, a store, and a few residences. Back of the blacksmith shop there was a sugar bush of hard maple trees.

In the sugar bush, each of the boys would try to do some stunt that none of the others would dare. They would swing from limb to limb or run along a branch far above ground, risking arms and legs in an effort to outdo their companions.

It was a common sight almost any evening to see a group of boys gathered about the anvil in the shop, trying to outlift one another. One of their favorite stunts was to try to lift the anvil by grasping the tapering end which is called the horn.

There were many kinds of contests among this group, some thought of on the spur of the moment and forgotten with the darkness. High jumping, wrestling, and fighting were natural boy activities that were not neglected. One sport that they all enjoyed was tug of war. On the wall of the blacksmith shop hung a long rope. This rope was used to hobble refractory horses when they were to be shod. To the boys, however, this rope was there for their use, and they were not backward in appropriating it.

Usually, during the evening, the boys played some kind of game in which most of the group joined. In their favorite game, "Duck on the Rock," one boy guarded his "duck" from the stones of the others; and the fun began as the boys gathered their stray shots. It was this game that was later to play such an important part in the origin of basketball.

The game of the evening finished, the boys filed down the dusty road, crossed the old rail fence into Anderson's pasture, and made their way to the swimming hole in the Indian River. It was typical boys' play in the water; they ducked one another and used the mud banks for a slippery slide. When it was dark, they left the river and went back to their homes, as each of them would arise with the sun the next morning.

As the summer waned and the maple trees turned brilliant colors, the activities of the boys changed. There were still contests at the Corners, but there were also days of hunting and fishing. It was rare sport to catch the great northern pike in the late fall, and the partridges and snowshoe hares were plentiful. Occasionally one of the men would bag a deer or a Canadian lynx; and at these times the boys would have something special to discuss in the evenings.

Sometime in November, the first freeze would come sweeping out of the North, and cold and snow would put a finish to the summer play. Not long after the first freeze there would be ice; and when the Indian River froze over there was skating. The old swimming hole was once more in use, the log fires burned every evening, as the sharp blades of the skates cut the glazed surface of the Indian River.

One of the boys of the Bennie's Corners group was an orphan who made his home with his uncle.

His father and mother had died when he was eight years of age. It was the first night of skating, and this boy stood by the fire on the river and watched the other fellows gliding over the ice. The lad did not have any skates, and he was too proud to ask his uncle to buy him a pair. He left the river and went to his uncle's shop, and there late into the night the neighbors saw a light burning.

The next evening, when the group gathered at the river, this young fellow was among them, and over his shoulders hung a pair of skates. These skates were not like those of the other boys, but were made from a pair of old files set firmly into strips of hickory wood. Years later, when necessity arose, this same inventive lad gave to the world not a pair of home-made skates, but the game of basketball.

Bob-sledding was a popular sport with this group, and many evenings boys and girls would pile into a sled filled with straw, and, singing and yelling, they would go from house to house, rousing out some of their friends who had failed to start with the group. Often the whole crowd would enter some kitchen to laugh and chatter as they ate doughnuts and drank cider.

Tobogganing and snowshoeing were other sports that they enjoyed in the winter. They built a long slide for the toboggans and spent many evenings whizzing down this slide at a speed that only a toboggan can attain.

Play, however, was not the only factor that affected the lives of these boys. Work had its influence as well. When a boy was sent into the field with a team, he was expected to accomplish the task that he had been assigned. If some emergency arose, he was not expected to go to the house and ask for help; if it were at all possible, he was expected to fix the trouble himself. Sometimes deep in the woods a singletree would break, and it was expected that the teamster, whether he be sixteen or sixty, make his own repairs.

Bennie's Corners was my home community, and my early training was with the group that I have described. Both at play and at work I was closely associated with the people of this district, and I recall distinctly some of the lessons that I learned as a boy.

One incident that I will never forget was my trip across the Misiwaka River for a load of hay. We had been using a crossing down the river, but rather than to go around, I decided that I would cross higher up. I went across the ice to the far shore, and quickly loaded my sleigh. I started back, and was almost to the home shore, when with a crash my team went into the water. We had hit a spring hole, and I did not have time to go for help. I can well remember the lump that arose in my throat. A valuable team of horses was struggling in the water, simply because I had been in too much of a hurry to go a quarter of a mile down the stream.

I did not have much time to think, for the team was threshing in the water and something had to be done. Luckily the sleigh had not gone in, and I rushed around to loosen the doubletrees. This helped the horses a little; one especially was kicking and floundering on one side of the hole. I loosed a rein, and throwing it over the horse's head, I began to tug with all my might. In a few moments the horse, after a desperate lunge, slipped up on the clear ice, and I quickly worked him away from the hole. In a few moments I had the other horse out of the water, and I sat down on the bank to rest a minute. As I turned to see if the horses were all right, I saw my uncle standing back in the trees, watching me. I never knew how long he had stood there, but I am sure that he was there before I had pulled the horses out.

The use of our own initiative was great training for us boys, and prepared us to meet our future problems. Some of us went to the city; others answered the call to new lands in western Canada.

It is surprising how well many of these country boys succeeded after leaving their boyhood home. Robert Tait McKenzie, the noted sculptor of athletes, went to McGill, then later to Philadelphia to the University of Pennsylvania as director of physical education. Jim Young entered medical school. Bob Toshack started a transport company in Winnipeg. Jack and Bob Steele built a canning factory in San Diego, California. Bill Naismith became a machinist and is now with the Denver Gardner people in Denver, Colorado. Gilbert Moir owned a hardware store in Arnprior, Ontario. Jack Snedden was a salesman in New York City. And as for myself, I went to Montreal to study for the ministry.

In the fall of 1883, I left Almonte to attend McGill University, in Montreal. I had been working on the farm for years, and my physical condition was excellent. It was with a firm determination and a great sense of confidence that I was to enter the study for the ministry. For several years I had been wondering what I wanted to accomplish; finally I decided that the only real satisfaction that I would ever derive from life was to help my fellow beings. At that time the ministry was the way that one attempted to help his fellows. I knew that there would be seven years before I would be able to go out into the world and begin my life work, but I felt that the time spent would be worth while.

I had earned a fellowship in McGill and had corresponded with the university authorities in regard to attending their school. When I reported to the dean of the college, I was told that my room had been selected for me and I was shown to the dormitory that was to be my home for the next few years.

I had missed several years during high school, and when I entered college I felt that I had little time to lose and was determined to study as hard as I could. I spent long hours over my books, and everything else was forgotten in my desire to finish my education and get into the field as soon as possible.

One evening, as I sat studying in my room, someone knocked at the door. I raised my head from the book and called, "Come in." Two juniors in the college, Jim McFarland and Donald Dewar, entered. I knew these fellows only to speak to them, and I was surprised at their visit. I asked them to sit down, and after some small conversation, McFarland turned to me and said:

"Naismith, we have been watching you for some time, and we see that you never take part in any of the activities. You spend too much time with your books."

I looked at McFarland with a smile. He was a big fellow, one of the outstanding athletes of the school. Then my gaze turned to Dewar. Dewar did not appear strong, and as he noticed my glance, he spoke:

"Believe me, Naismith, what McFarland says is true. I wouldn't listen to the fellows either, and you see the results."

The fellows talked for some time, and finally, as they started to leave, I explained to them that I was grateful for their advice, but I was sure that I was strong enough to study as hard as I wanted to and that I did not have time for sports.

Late that night, when I had finished my studies and lay on my bed, I began to wonder why those two fellows had seen fit to spend their time in giving advice to a freshman. The more I thought, the more clearly to my mind came the realization that they were doing it purely for my own benefit. I determined that the next day I would go over to the gymnasium and see what they were doing.

It was the next afternoon that I went, and from that time to the present I have been engaged in physical work both in the gymnasium and on the athletic field.

Though my introduction to gymnastics in the university came about in a casual way, my entrance into athletics was accidental. One evening, on my way home from a trip down town with a chum, I stopped to watch the football team at practice. During the scrimmage, the center had his nose broken, and there was no substitute to take his place.

The captain called out, "Won't one of you fellows come in and help us out?"

No one responded immediately, and throwing off my coat, I volunteered to take his place. At the close of practice, the captain asked me if I would fill the center position the next Saturday in a game with Queen's University. I purchased a suit—at that time each man bought his own equipment—and played my first game of college football. For seven years I played without missing a game and enjoyed the sport, even though it was not thought proper for a "theolog." Football at that time was supposed to be a tool of the devil, and it was much to my amusement that I learned that some of my comrades gathered in one of the rooms one evening to pray for my soul.

It was in my senior year in theology that the

incident occurred that changed my career from the profession of the ministry to that of athletics, which was then in its infancy and rather in disrepute.

During a hotly contested football game, the guard on my left encountered some difficulty, and losing his temper he made some remarks that, though forceful, are unprintable. When he had cooled a little, he leaned over to me and whispered, "I beg your pardon, Jim; I forgot you were there."

This surprised me more than a little. I had never said a word about his profanity, and I could not understand why he should have apologized to me. Later, thinking the matter over, the only reason that I could give for the guard's action was that I played the game with all my might and yet held myself under control.

A few days later I went down to the Y.M.C.A. and told my experiences to the secretary, Mr. D. A. Budge. In our conversation I brought up the point that I thought that there might be other effective ways of doing good besides preaching. After a while Budge told me that there was a school in Springfield, Massachusetts, that was developing men for this field. I made up my mind that I would drop the ministry and go into this other work.

On consulting with my favorite professor, I received some very sound advice. He said, "Naismith, I can't tell you what you should do. While this new field appears good, I would finish the course in theology; then if you do not like this new work, you can return to your original field."

I followed the professor's counsel, and have had frequent occasion to be thankful for it.

After graduating from the theological college, I spent the summer visiting Y.M.C.A.'s in the United States, spending a few days at the summer school in Springfield. It was there that I first met Dr. Luther Gulick.

On arriving unannounced at Springfield, I went to the Training School and asked for the dean of the physical education department. I was informed that Dr. Gulick was in class but would be out shortly. I sat down and waited.

I had been brought up in a British university, where all the professors with whom I was acquainted were elderly men, sedate and dignified. After I had waited a few minutes, a man about my own age entered the office. He was tall and angular, his eyes were a bright piercing blue, and his hair and whiskers were a peculiar shade of carroty red. This man crossed the room with a rapid, jerky stride, fingered the mail on his desk, and then crossed to where I sat. With a winning smile on his face and a freckled hand extended, he welcomed me to the school. It is little wonder that I immediately felt a warm regard for Dr. Gulick, and I knew that, with this man as dean of the school, I was going to enjoy my work. I told him of my experiences and convictions as we chatted.

When the next class period started, he invited me to attend the session. I was delighted with Dr. Gulick's methods of teaching; he seemed to take the students into his confidence as he discussed the subject with them. Later, I was to find that he was one of the few men whose teachings have remained with me and have been a help not only in my profession but in my life as well.

By appointment we met that evening and sat for hours discussing ideas that were of common interest. He was engaged at that time in planning a pentathlon for the Y.M.C.A. As we talked, he convinced me, more and more, of the importance of the work of a physical director.

The rest of the summer was spent at my old home in Almonte. In the fall I started for Springfield, and in Ottawa I was joined by T. D. Patton. In Montreal, Dave Corbett met us, and we three formed the Canadian contingent at the International Training School at Springfield, Massachusetts.

On arriving at the school, I met A. A. Stagg,

who had been a theological student at Yale, and who had come to Springfield inspired with the same ideals that had brought me from McGill. I had gone into Dr. Gulick's office and found him seated at his desk talking to a short stocky man of my own age. Gulick looked up and motioned for me to come over. He arose with his usual quick manner and introduced me to the man who was to be a fellow student for one year and a teaching colleague for another, Amos Alonzo Stagg. Stagg grasped my hand with a grip that he was accustomed to use on a baseball, and I retaliated with a grasp that I had learned in wrestling. Each of us, through Dr. Gulick, had heard of the other, but this was our first meeting; our friendship has lasted more than forty years.

It was a few days after enrollment in the fall that Dr. Gulick conceived the idea of starting football in the school. Stagg had been an all-American at Yale, Bond and Black had played at Knox College, and I had played seven years of English Rugby at McGill. Stagg was appointed coach, and he selected thirteen men and asked them to purchase suits. I had the Rugby suit that I had used at McGill, and I laughed at the others when they purchased long-sleeved canvas jackets. My suit resembled a track suit; it was only a few days later that I sheepishly bought one of the long-sleeved jackets like the others. The only remnant of my McGill uniform that I retained was the red and white striped stockings.

On the football field, I really learned to know Stagg and to admire his methods. He was the same then as he is today. Just before the opening game I had my first view of the real man who, through the years, has become the dean of American football. It was in the dressing room, just before we were to go out on the field. Stagg had given us our instructions; then he turned to us,

"Let us ask God's blessing on our game."

He did not pray for victory, but he prayed that each man should do his best and show the true Christian spirit.

For two years it was his custom to ask different members of the team to lead; during those two years I never heard anything but the same spirit breathed by the men. Our team averaged less than one hundred sixty pounds, but we played games with Harvard, Yale, Amherst, and other large colleges. We won our share of the games, and our team became known as "Stagg's Stubby Christians."

I recognized Stagg's ability as a coach, and noticed that he would pick one man for a position and keep him there. He seemed to have the uncanny ability to place the right man in the right position. I asked him one day how it happened that he played me at center. Stagg looked at me, and in a serious voice replied:

"Jim, I play you at center because you can do the meanest things in the most gentlemanly manner."

At the end of the first year, Stagg and I were retained on the faculty; and it was during the following year that the opportunity came to me to invent the game of basketball.

CHAPTER II

THE NEED OF A NEW GAME

DURING the summer of 1891, the need for some new game became imperative. From many different states the young men had gathered for the summer term of the Springfield training school. No matter where they came from, these directors complained that the members of the gymnasium classes were losing interest in the type of work that had been introduced by R. J. Roberts, at one time a circus performer. Tired of the spectacular stunts, Roberts had inaugurated a system of exercise that he had termed body-building work, intended largely to develop physique, health, and vigor, with little thought for the interest of the participant. Body-building work consisted of light and heavy apparatus exercise based on the German system, but excluded many of the stunts that were performed by the expert gymnast. Those directors who had been trained under Roberts' leadership found it difficult to attract young men to their classes.

In the late seventies, college students had begun
to take an interest in intercollegiate sports, especially track and football. These games had become
firmly established, and many of the more active
students took part in them. When the men who
engaged in these sports went to the city to enter
business and found that they had leisure time, it
was only natural that they should look for some
kind of athletic diversion. In an effort to find it,
they joined the athletic clubs, the bicycle clubs, the
Y.M.C.A., and other organizations of this type.
During the winter season these clubs had nothing
to offer in the way of athletics, but tried to interest
the men in gymnastics.

The former college men were natural leaders in
their communities. When they compared the thrills
of football with those of mass and squad gymnastics,
they were frankly discontented. The expert gymnast got all the excitement from a perfect per-
formance of a daring stunt and the football player
from winning an intercollegiate contest. What
this new generation wanted was pleasure and thrill
rather than physical benefits. The summer school
students freely discussed these conditions. No one,
however, seemed to be able to offer a solution to the
problem.

Doctor Gulick was working desperately on the

problem that seemed to threaten the whole subject of physical training, especially in the Y.M.C.A. He recognized the fact that something new had to be introduced, but he saw only the mountaintops, forgetting the valleys that lay between. He was impatient with those who would not fly to the summit.

It seemed to me that Gulick and I made a good team, for he was always an inspiration to me. In one discussion, he saw a vision of some project, and I suggested that the thing to do was to begin in a remote way to reach the point.

Gulick said, "Naismith, you are nothing but an obstructionist."

I understood his attitude and answered, "I am not an obstructionist, but a pathfinder."

At this remark, we both laughed.

Doctor Gulick looked to other countries for a solution. I was sent to Martha's Vineyard, Massachusetts, to study the principles of the Swedish system, then being taught by Baron Nils Posse.

On my arrival, I explained to Posse what I was seeking. He at once became interested. Even though it was contrary to the principles of Swedish gymnastics, he recognized the need of some form of recreation for the Y.M.C.A. Baron Posse told me which courses in his school would best suit my purpose. The work in the school was new to me, and I enjoyed the change. I admired the results in the posture, poise, and alertness that were developed in the students and displayed by the instructors.

The summer school at Martha's Vineyard finished, I returned to Springfield to report my findings to Dr. Gulick. I told him that there were many valuable factors in the Swedish system— some of which we afterward adopted—but that it did not solve our problem.

This was the third time that Dr. Gulick had received a like report about foreign systems. The German system had been thoroughly tried; the French system had failed to help us; and now the Swedish system offered no relief. It became evident that we would be forced to solve our own problem rather than fall back on any system that was then in use.

At the opening of the regular school session in the fall of 1891, Dr. Gulick introduced a new course, a seminar in psychology. Among the members of this class were Dr. F. N. Seerley, Dr. Robert A. Clark, Dr. A. T. Halstead, A. A. Stagg, and myself.

At our meetings, many questions of physical education were discussed. Among these was the need for some game that would be interesting, easy to learn, and easy to play in the winter and by artificial light.

During the discussion of inventions, Dr. Gulick made the statement: "There is nothing new under the sun. All so-called new things are simply recombinations of the factors of things that are now in existence." The doctor used as an illustration the recombining of elements to make new chemical substances, such as synthetic drugs and dyes.

Mentally applying this principle to our need for a new game, I made the remark: "Doctor, if that is so, we can invent a new game that will meet our needs. All that we have to do is to take the factors of our known games and recombine them, and we will have the game we are looking for."

With his characteristic quickness, Dr. Gulick asked the class to try out my idea and to bring a plan for a new game to the next session. Little did I think at that time what effect my suggestion would have in the field of sports and on my own life. Each one of us went his way with the firm conviction that at the next meeting he would have solved the problem and given to the world a new game. The following week, when the group met, none of us had anything to offer. We had all been so busy in trying to get results from our regular work that we had found little time to plan for something new.

The fact that this was assigned to us as a problem has led to the statement sometimes made that basketball was invented in one night. It was many weeks later that basketball actually came into existence.

When the fall sports were ended, our attention was again called to the conditions which had previously caused us so much worry. The school at that time was training two classes of leaders, one as physical directors and the other as secretaries.

During the football season, both of these groups worked together. The two guards, an end, and a halfback were from the secretarial department; the rest of the team was from the physical directors' group. At the close of the outdoor sports, all the students went to the gymnasium for their exercise. The physical directors and the secretaries did their work in separate classes. The first were interested in getting as much as possible out of their regular class work, because it trained them for their profession. It was comparatively easy to teach this group. The secretaries, however, had a different attitude toward physical activities; they had all the physical development they needed and were not interested. They were, nevertheless, required to spend an hour each day in what was to most of them distasteful work.

The instructor assigned to the secretaries' class was Dr. A. T. Halstead, an expert in marching and mass calisthenics, and it was only natural that he should stress these activities. Try as he might, he could arouse little enthusiasm for this kind of work, and he realized that the men were even developing an antipathy toward exercise of all kinds. At the next meeting of the faculty, Dr. Halstead requested that he be given some other class. Dr. R. A. Clark was then assigned to the class.

Clark was the best gymnast and athlete in the faculty, a Phi Beta Kappa of Williams College, and a Doctor of Medicine. He was thoroughly prepared to teach any class in the school. He began his work with a great deal of enthusiasm. His first step was to drop all marching and calisthenics and to take up apparatus work, mixing in such athletic events as could be carried on in a space sixty-five by forty-five feet. Here again the men were given exercise in which they had no interest. Try as hard as he could, Clark failed to arouse any enthusiasm for the work that had been intensely interesting to the classes he had taught before.

It soon became evident that the antagonism of the class toward physical work was increasing; at the next meeting of the faculty, Dr. Clark said that no one could do anything with that group. While we were discussing this condition, I again spoke my mind, saying: "The trouble is not with the men but with the system that we are using. The kind of work for this particular class should be of a recreative nature, something that would appeal to their play instincts."

While this statement was true, it did not help, as once more we were faced with the same old question. What could we give them? There was no indoor game that would invoke the enthusiasm of football or baseball. The only indoor games that we had at that time were three-deep, prisoners' base, long-ball, and games of this type. It is easy to see now why it was impossible to interest grown men in the games that even the youngsters today fail to enjoy.

The group in the faculty meeting was quiet; each was trying to think of a solution. It was like a bolt of lightning from a clear sky when Dr. Gulick turned to me and said, "Naismith, I want you to take that class and see what you can do with it."

Knowing the difficulty of the task that was being assigned to me, I immediately began to make excuses and to show why I should be left with the classes that I was teaching at that time. I had been instructing in boxing, wrestling, swimming, and canoeing, all sports that I felt proficient in and liked. Gymnastics did not appeal to me as the sports did, and I tried my best to dissuade Dr. Gulick from changing my work. His mind was made up, however; it mattered little how much I talked: my fate was sealed, and I was to take the class. I had little sympathy for the class that had disposed of two instructors and was waiting for another.

As we left the meeting, Dr. Gulick noticed my attitude, and falling into step beside me, walked down the hall. We had almost reached his office when he turned to me and said,

"Naismith, now would be a good time for you to work on that new game that you said could be invented."

When he had assigned me the class of incorrigibles, I had felt that I was being imposed on; but when he told me to do what all the directors of the country had failed to accomplish, I felt it was the last straw. My fist closed, and I looked up into Gulick's face. I saw there only a quizzical smile. There was little left for me to do but to accept the challenge.

I have never found out whether it was intentional on the part of Dr. Gulick to unite the two difficulties, or merely incidental, to get rid of two vexing problems, that he gave both of them to the same person; but it is certain that they worked together for ultimate good.

The class was led by two business men, Patton and Mahan, and whatever met with their approval would be accepted by the rest of the group. Had they been satisfied with my first attempt, basketball would not have been originated.

I learned to appreciate the attitude of the class that I had been given; they were older men, and I felt that if I were in their place, I would probably have done all I could to get rid of the obnoxious requirements. This fellow feeling may have been of assistance to me in my task.

Following out the suggestion that I had made in the faculty meeting, I began by laying aside all heavy work, using only the games that we had been accustomed to play for recreation after the regular class work. These games relieved the men of the drudgery of which they had complained; but fifteen minutes of a game like three deep became more monotonous than work on the parallel bars. Ten minutes of sailors' tag gave them plenty of exercise—but what were we to do during the other thirty minutes?

All of the gymnastic games proved to be the same, and the games that had been worked out by

others proved as ineffective. Doctor Sargent, of
Harvard, had started a game called battle-ball, and
Dr. Gulick originated two games, one a modification of ante-over with a medicine ball and the other
a modification of cricket. I tried all these games
but was forced to abandon them because they did
not retain the interest of the class. I then determined to modify some of the outdoor sports.

Football was the first game that I modified. In
eliminating the roughness, I tried to substitute the
tackling of English Rugby for that of the American game. In Rugby, the tackle must be made
above the hips, and the endeavor is to stop the runner rather than to throw him. The changing of the
tackle did not appeal to the members of the class,
who had been taught to throw the runner with as
much force as possible, so that if he were able to
get up at all, he would at least be in a dazed condition. To ask these men to handle their opponents gently was to make their favorite sport a
laughing stock, and they would have none of it.

Soccer, or as it was then called, Association football, was the game that I next attempted to modify.
On the gymnasium floor the men were accustomed
to wearing soft soled shoes, and I thought, therefore, they would use caution in kicking the ball.
Many of the class had played soccer outdoors, and

when they saw an opening for a goal, they forgot all about their shoes and drove the ball with all their might. As a result of this, many of them went limping off the floor; instead of an indoor soccer game, we had a practical lesson in first aid.

Some of the former soccer players had learned to drive the ball with the inside of the foot; and if they missed their shots at the goal, they were likely to smash the windows, which were at that time unscreened. There were times when the game waxed so furious that it was necessary to call time out, in order that we could remove the clubs and the dumbbells that were knocked from the racks on the wall.

The reaction of the boys toward soccer was, to say the least, unfavorable, and we soon dropped the attempt to change soccer into an indoor game. I had pinned my hopes on these two games, and when they failed me, there seemed little chance of success. Each attempt was becoming more difficult.

There was still one more game that I was determined to try, and this was the Canadian game of lacrosse. I had played lacrosse as a boy, and to some extent in the university. Later I had been associated with the Shamrocks, a professional team in Montreal. I have always considered this the best of all games, but it seemed impossible to make an indoor sport of one that required so much space.

The only modification that I could think of was to eliminate or to modify the crosse. I thought of making a short, one-handed crosse, somewhat like a ping-pong racquet, but there was neither time nor money to manufacture it. As I was not willing to give up the game without a trial, I used the regular crosse.

In the group there were seven Canadians; and when these men put into practice some of the tricks they had been taught in the outdoor game, football and soccer appeared tame in comparison. No bones were broken in the game, but faces were scarred and hands were hacked. Those who had never played the game were unfortunate, for it was these men to whom the flying crosses did the most damage. The beginners were injured and the experts were disgusted; another game went into the discard.

CHAPTER III

THE ORIGIN OF
BASKETBALL

TWO weeks had almost passed since I had taken over the troublesome class. The time was almost gone; in a day or two I would have to report to the faculty the success or failure of my attempts. So far they had all been failures, and it seemed to me that I had exhausted my resources. The prospect before me was, to say the least, discouraging. How I hated the thought of going back to the group and admitting that, after all my theories, I, too, had failed to hold the interest of the class. It was worse than losing a game. All the stubbornness of my Scotch ancestry was aroused, all my pride of achievement urged me on; I would not go back and admit that I had failed.

The day before my two weeks ended I met the class. I will always remember that meeting. I had nothing new to try and no idea of what I was going to do. The class period passed with little order, and at the end of the hour the boys left the gym. I can still see that group of fellows filing out the door. As that last pair of grey pants vanished into the locker room, I saw the end of all my ambitions and hopes.

With weary footsteps I mounted the flight of narrow stairs that led to my office directly over the locker room. I slumped down in my chair, my head in my hands and my elbows on the desk. I was a thoroughly disheartened and discouraged young instructor. Below me, I could hear the boys in the locker room having a good time; they were giving expression to the very spirit that I had tried so hard to evoke.

I had been a student the year before, and I could picture the group in that locker room. A towel would snap and some fellow would jerk erect and try to locate the guilty individual. Some of it was rough play, but it was all in fun, and each of them entered into it with that spirit. There would be talking and jesting, and I could even imagine the things that the group would be saying about my efforts. I was sure that the fellows did not dislike me, but I was just as sure that they felt that I had given them nothing better than the other instructors.

As I listened to the noise in the room below, my discouragement left me. I looked back over my attempts to see, if possible, the cause of my failures. I passed in review the gymnastic games that I had tried, and I saw that they were impossible. They were really children's games; the object that was to be obtained changed with each play, and no man could be interested in this type of game. It was necessary to have some permanent objective that would keep the minds of the participants active and interested.

As I thought of the other games that I had tried, I realized that the normal individual is strongly influenced by tradition. If he is interested in a game, any attempt to modify that game sets up an antagonism in his mind. I realized that any attempt to change the known games would necessarily result in failure. It was evident that a new principle was necessary; but how to evolve this principle was beyond my ken.

As I sat there at my desk, I began to study games from the philosophical side. I had been taking one game at a time and had failed to find what I was looking for. This time I would take games as a whole and study them.

My first generalization was that all team games used a ball of some kind; therefore, any new game must have a ball. Two kinds of balls were used at that time, one large and the other small. I noted

that all games that used a small ball had some intermediate equipment with which to handle it. Cricket
and baseball had bats, lacrosse and hockey had
sticks, tennis and squash had rackets. In each of
these games, the use of the intermediate equipment
made the game more difficult to learn. The Americans were at sea with a lacrosse stick, and the
Canadians could not use a baseball bat.

The game that we sought would be played by
many; therefore, it must be easy to learn. Another
objection to a small ball was that it could be easily
hidden. It would be difficult for a group to play a
game in which the ball was in sight only part of
the time.

I then considered a large ball that could be easily
handled and which almost anyone could catch and
throw with very little practice. I decided that the
ball should be large and light, one that could be
easily handled and yet could not be concealed.
There were two balls of this kind then in use, one
the spheroid of Rugby and the other the round ball
of soccer. It was not until later that I decided
which one of these two I would select.

The type of a ball being settled, I turned next to
the point of interest of various games. I concluded
that the most interesting game at that time was
American Rugby. I asked myself why this game

could not be used as an indoor sport. The answer to this was easy. It was because tackling was necessary in Rugby. But why was tackling necessary? Again the answer was easy. It was because the men were allowed to run with the ball, and it was necessary to stop them. With these facts in mind, I sat erect at my desk and said aloud:

"If he can't run with the ball, we don't have to tackle; and if we don't have to tackle, the roughness will be eliminated."

I can still recall how I snapped my fingers and shouted,

"I've got it!"

This time I felt that I really had a new principle for a game, one that would not violate any tradition. On looking back, it was hard to see why I was so elated. I had as yet nothing but a single idea, but I was sure that the rest would work out correctly.

Starting with the idea that the player in possession of the ball could not run with it, the next step was to see just what he could do with it. There was little choice in this respect. It would be necessary for him to throw it or bat it with his hand. In my mind, I began to play a game and to visualize the movements of the players. Suppose that a player was running, and a teammate threw the ball to him.

D'Ambra

BENNIE'S CORNERS, 1882

D'Ambra

SPRINGFIELD, 1892

Realizing that it would be impossible for him to stop immediately, I made this exception: when a man was running and received the ball, he must make an honest effort to stop or else pass the ball immediately. This was the second step of the game.

In my mind I was still sticking to the traditions of the older games, especially football. In that game, the ball could be thrown in any direction except forward. In this new game, however, the player with the ball could not advance, and I saw no reason why he should not be allowed to throw or bat it in any direction. So far, I had a game that was played with a large light ball; the players could not run with the ball, but must pass it or bat it with the hands; and the pass could be made in any direction.

As I mentally played the game, I remembered that I had seen two players in a soccer game, both after the ball. One player attempted to head the ball just as the other player kicked at it. The result was a badly gashed head for the first man. I then turned this incident to the new game. I could imagine one player attempting to strike the ball with his fist and, intentionally or otherwise, coming in contact with another player's face. I then decided that the fist must not be used in striking the ball.

The game now had progressed only to the point where it was "keep away," and my experience with gymnastic games convinced me that it would not hold the interest of the players.

The next step was to devise some objective for the players. In all existing games there was some kind of a goal, and I felt that this was essential. I thought of the different games, in the hope that I might be able to use one of their goals. Football had a goal line, over which the ball must be carried, and goal posts, over which the ball might be kicked. Soccer, lacrosse, and hockey had goals into which the ball might be driven. Tennis and badminton had marks on the court inside which the ball must be kept. Thinking of all these, I mentally placed a goal like the one used in lacrosse at each end of the floor.

A lacrosse goal is simply a space six feet high and eight feet wide. The players attempt to throw the ball into this space; the harder the ball is thrown, the more chance to make a goal. I was sure that this play would lead to roughness, and I did not want that. I thought of limiting the sweep of the arms or of having the ball delivered from in front of the person, but I knew that many would resent my limiting the power of the player.

By what line of association it occurred to me I

do not know, but I was back in Bennie's Corners, Ontario, playing Duck on the Rock. I could remember distinctly the large rock back of the blacksmith shop, about as high as our knees and as large around as a wash tub. Each of us would get a "duck," a stone about as large as our two doubled fists. About twenty feet from the large rock we would draw a base line, and then in various manners we would choose one of the group to be guard, or "it."

To start the game, the guard placed his duck on the rock, and we behind the base line attempted to knock it off by throwing our ducks. More often than not, when we threw our ducks we missed, and if we went to retrieve them, the guard tagged us; then one of us had to change places with him. If, however, someone knocked the guard's "duck" off the rock, he had to replace it before he could tag anyone.

It came distinctly to my mind that some of the boys threw their ducks as hard as they could; when they missed, the ducks were far from the base. When they went to retrieve them, they had farther to run and had more chance of being tagged. On the other hand, if the duck was tossed in an arc, it did not go so far. If the guard's duck was hit, it fell on the far side of the rock, whereas the one that was thrown bounced nearer the base and was easily caught up before the guard replaced his. When the duck was thrown in an arc, accuracy was more effective than force.

With this game in mind, I thought that if the goal were horizontal instead of vertical, the players would be compelled to throw the ball in an arc; and force, which made for roughness, would be of no value.

A horizontal goal, then, was what I was looking for, and I pictured it in my mind. I would place a box at either end of the floor, and each time the ball entered the box it would count as a goal. There was one thing, however, that I had overlooked. If nine men formed a defense around the goal, it would be impossible for the ball to enter it; but if I placed the goal above the players' heads, this type of defense would be useless. The only chance that the guards would have would be to go out and get the ball before the opponents had an opportunity to throw for goal.

I had a team game with equipment and an objective. My problem now was how to start it. Again I reviewed the games with which I was familiar. I found that the intent of starting any game was to give each side an equal chance to obtain the ball. I thought of water polo, where the teams were lined up at the ends of the pool and at a signal the ball was thrown into the center. There was always a mad scramble to gain possession of the ball, and it took only an instant for me to reject this plan. I could see nine men at each end of the gym, all making a rush for the ball as it was thrown into the center of the floor; and I winced as I thought of the results of that collision.

I then turned to the game of English Rugby. When the ball went out of bounds on the side line, it was taken by the umpire and thrown in between two lines of forward players. This was somewhat like polo, but the players had no chance to run at each other. As I thought of this method of starting the game, I remembered one incident that happened to me. In a game with Queen's College, the ball was thrown between the two lines of players. I took one step and went high in the air. I got the ball all right, but as I came down I landed on a shoulder that was shoved into my midriff. I decided that this method would not do. I did feel, though, that if the roughness could be eliminated, that tossing up the ball between two teams was the fairest way of starting a game. I reasoned that if I picked only one player from each team and threw the ball up between them, there would be little chance for roughness. I realize now how seriously

I underestimated the ingenuity of the American boy.

When I had decided how I would start the game, I felt that I would have little trouble. I knew that there would be questions to be met; but I had the fundamental principles of a game, and I was more than willing to try to meet these problems. I continued with my day's work, and it was late in the evening before I again had a chance to think of my new scheme. I believe that I am the first person who ever played basketball; and although I used the bed for a court, I certainly played a hard game that night.

The following morning I went into my office, thinking of the new game. I had not yet decided what ball I should use. Side by side on the floor lay two balls, one a football and the other a soccer ball.

I noticed the lines of the football and realized that it was shaped so that it might be carried in the arms. There was to be no carrying of the ball in this new game, so I walked over, picked up the soccer ball, and started in search of a goal.

As I walked down the hall, I met Mr. Stebbins, the superintendent of buildings. I asked him if he had two boxes about eighteen inches square. Stebbins thought a minute, and then said:

"No, I haven't any boxes, but I'll tell you what I do have. I have two old peach baskets down in the store room, if they will do you any good."

I told him to bring them up, and a few minutes later he appeared with the two baskets tucked under his arm. They were round and somewhat larger at the top than at the bottom. I found a hammer and some nails and tacked the baskets to the lower rail of the balcony, one at either end of the gym.

I was almost ready to try the new game, but I felt that I needed a set of rules, in order that the men would have some guide. I went to my office, pulled out a scratch pad, and set to work. The rules were so clear in my mind that in less than an hour I took my copy to Miss Lyons, our stenographer, who typed the following set of thirteen rules.

The ball to be an ordinary *Association* football.

1. The ball may be thrown in any direction with one or both hands.

2. The ball may be batted in any direction with one or both hands (never with the fist).

3. A player cannot run with the ball. The player must throw it from the spot on which he catches it; allowance to be made for a man who catches the ball when running at a good speed.

4. The ball must be held in or between the

hands; the arms or body must not be used for holding it.

5. No shouldering, holding, pushing, tripping, or striking, in any way the person of an opponent shall be allowed; the first infringement of this rule by any person shall count as a foul, the second shall disqualify him until the next goal is made, or, if there was evident intent to injure the person for the whole of the game, no substitute allowed.

6. A foul is striking at the ball with the fist, violation of Rules 3, 4, and such as described in Rule 5.

7. If either side makes three consecutive fouls, it shall count a goal for the opponents. (Consecutive means without the opponents in the meantime making a foul.)

8. A goal shall be made when the ball is thrown or batted from the grounds into the basket and stays there, providing those defending the goal do not touch or disturb the goal. If the ball rests on the edge and the opponent moves the basket, it shall count as a goal.

9. When the ball goes out of bounds, it shall be thrown into the field and played by the person first touching it. In case of a dispute, the umpire shall throw it straight into the field. The thrower-in is allowed five seconds. If he holds it longer it shall go to the opponent. If any side persists in delaying the game, the umpire shall call a foul on them.

10. The umpire shall be judge of the men and shall note the fouls and notify the referee when three consecutive fouls have been made. He shall have power to disqualify men according to Rule 5.

11. The referee shall be judge of the ball and shall decide when the ball is in play, in bounds, to which side it belongs, and shall keep the time. He shall decide when a goal has been made, and keep account of the goals, with any other duties that are usually performed by a referee.

12. The time shall be two fifteen minute halves, with five minutes rest between.

13. The side making the most goals in that time shall be declared the winners. In case of a draw, the game may, by agreement of the captains, be continued until another goal is made.

When Miss Lyons finished typing the rules, it was almost class time, and I was anxious to get down to the gym. I took the rules and made my way down the stairs. Just inside the door there was a bulletin board for notices. With thumb tacks I fastened the rules to this board and then walked across the gym. I was sure in my own mind that the game was good, but it needed a real test. I felt that its success or failure depended largely on the way that the class received it.

The first member of the class to arrive was Frank Mahan. He was a southerner from North Carolina, had played tackle on the football team, and was the ringleader of the group. He saw me standing with a ball in my hand and perhaps surmised that another experiment was to be tried. He looked up at the basket on one end of the gallery, and then his eyes turned to me. He gazed at me for an instant, and then looked toward the other end of the gym. Perhaps I was nervous, because his exclamation sounded like a death knell as he said,

"Huh! another new game!"

When the class arrived, I called the roll and told them that I had another game, which I felt sure would be good. I promised them that if this was a failure, I would not try any more experiments. I then read the rules from the bulletin board and proceeded to organize the game.

There were eighteen men in the class; I selected two captains and had them choose sides. When the teams were chosen, I placed the men on the floor. There were three forwards, three centers, and three backs on each team. I chose two of the center men to jump, then threw the ball between them. It was the start of the first basketball game and the finish of the trouble with that class.

As was to be expected, they made a great many fouls at first; and as a foul was penalized by putting the offender on the side lines until the next goal was made, sometimes half of a team would be in the penalty area. It was simply a case of no one knowing just what to do. There was no team work, but each man did his best. The forwards tried to make goals and the backs tried to keep the opponents from making them. The team was large, and the floor was small. Any man on the field was close enough to the basket to throw for goal, and most of them were anxious to score. We tried, however, to develop team work by having the guards pass the ball to the forwards.

The game was a success from the time that the first ball was tossed up. The players were interested and seemed to enjoy the game. Word soon got around that they were having fun in Naismith's gym class, and only a few days after the first game we began to have a gallery.

The class met at eleven-thirty in the morning, and the game was in full swing by twelve o'clock. Some teachers from the Buckingham Grade School were passing the gym one day, and hearing the noise, decided to investigate. They could enter the gallery through a door that led to the street. Each day after that, they stopped to watch the game, sometimes becoming so interested that they would not have time to get their lunch. These teachers came to me one day and asked me why girls could not play that game. I told them that I saw no reason why they should not, and this group organized the first girls' basketball team.

It is little wonder that the crowd enjoyed the game. If we could see it today as it was played then, we would laugh too. The players were all mature men; most of them had mustaches, and one or two had full beards. Their pants were long, and their shirts had short sleeves. Sometimes when a player received the ball, he would poise with it over his head to make sure that he would make the goal. About the time that he was ready to throw, somone would reach up from behind and take the ball out of his hands. This occurred frequently and was a never-ending source of amusement. No matter how often a player lost the ball in this manner, he would always look around with a surprised expression that would plainly say, "Who did that?" His embarrassment only added to the laughter of the crowd.

It was shortly after the first game that Frank Mahan came to me before class hour and said:

"You remember the rules that were put on the bulletin board?"

"Yes, I do," I answered.

"They disappeared," he said.

"I know it," I replied.

"Well, I took them," Frank said. "I knew that this game would be a success, and I took them as a souvenir, but I think now that you should have them."

Mahan told me that the rules were in his trunk and that he would bring them down later. That afternoon he entered my office and handed me the two typewritten sheets. I still have them, and they are one of my prized possessions.

At the Christmas vacation a number of the students went home and some of them started the game in their local Y.M.C.A.'s. There were no printed rules at that time, and each student played the game as he remembered it. It was not until January, 1892, that the school paper, called the *Triangle,* first printed the rules under the heading, "A New Game."

One day after the students returned from their vacation, the same Frank Mahan came to me and asked me what I was going to call the game. I told him that I had not thought of the matter but was interested only in getting it started. Frank insisted that it must have a name and suggested the name of Naismith ball. I laughed and told him that I thought that name would kill any game. Frank then said:

"Why not call it basketball?"

"We have a basket and a ball, and it seems to me that would be a good name for it," I replied. It was in this way that basketball was named.

When the first game had ended, I felt that I could now go to Doctor Gulick and tell him that I had accomplished the two seemingly impossible tasks that he had assigned to me: namely, to interest the class in physical exercise and to invent a new game.

CHAPTER IV

CHANGES IN THE GAME

THE two questions that I am most commonly asked when I am discussing basketball with persons whom I have just met are, "How did you come to think of it?" and "What changes have taken place in the game since its origin?" I have attempted in the earlier chapters of the book to answer that first question, and in this chapter I shall endeavor to answer the second one.

To describe each minute change that has taken place in the game would be uninteresting and monotonous. Rather than do this I have selected some of the more important factors and have noted the changes in them. In the years since basketball was started, the interest in the game has grown far beyond anything that we could have imagined when it was originated. It is very gratifying to me that, in spite of its spread and development, there have been no changes in the fundamental principles on which the game was founded.

Many of the plays and maneuvers that we often

consider recent developments were really executed from the first. It is true that these plays are different today from what they were then, but that difference comes from the skill with which they are executed rather than from any change in principle.

In the process of planning the game, I decided that certain fundamental principles were necessary. These were five in number:

1. There must be a ball; it should be large, light, and handled with the hands.

2. There shall be no running with the ball.

3. No man on either team shall be restricted from getting the ball at any time that it is in play.

4. Both teams are to occupy the same area, yet there is to be no personal contact.

5. The goal shall be horizontal and elevated.

These five principles are still the unchanging factors of basketball.

Several rules have been added and others modified to meet the new conditions that have arisen from time to time, until the original thirteen rules are today embodied in some two hundred fifty-two statements.

It will be surprising to many to know how little the game has really changed throughout the years. People often believe that much of basketball is comparatively new, whereas in reality, the things that goal.

9. When the ball goes out of bounds it shall be thrown into the field, and played by the person first touching it. In case of a dispute the umpire shall throw it straight into the field. The thrower is allowed five seconds, if he holds it longer it shall go to the opponent. If any side persists in delaying the game, the umpire shall call a foul on them.

10. The umpire shall be judge of the men, and shall note the fouls, and notify the referee when three consecutive fouls have been made. He shall have power to disqualify men according to Rule 5.

11. The referee shall be judge of the ball and shall decide when the ball is in play, in bounds, and to which side it belongs, and shall keep the time. He shall decide when a goal has been made, and keep account of the goals with any other duties that are usually performed by a referee.

12. The time shall be two fifteen minutes halves, with five minutes rest between.

13. The side making the most goals in that time shall be declared the winners. In case of a draw the game may, by agreement of the captains, be continued until another goal is made.

First draft of Basket Ball rules- thing in the gym that the boys might learn the rules - Feb. 1892

A PAGE FROM THE FIRST DRAFT OF THE RULES

THE FIRST BASKETBALL TEAM—NOTE THE BASKETS
The International Y.M.C.A. Training School, 1892

have been considered of recent development were embodied in the game almost from its conception.

When the question is asked, "What is the biggest change in basketball?" it is easy for me to answer. There is no doubt in my mind that it is in the skill of the players and the kind of plays that have been adopted. At first, anyone played the game, and it was entirely possible for some mature individual to begin and to play in match games. Today boys are brought up playing basketball, and it is little wonder that the degree of skill of the players is the outstanding change that has taken place in the game. Formerly, the players were trained and coached over a period of three or four years. Today that training may cover ten years, and frequently more.

Changes in the Plays

1. *The Dribble.* In discussing some of the specific changes that have taken place, it may be well to take up first one of the most spectacular and exciting maneuvers in basketball, the dribble. It is really as old as the game, and the changes that have taken place are merely developments.

The dribble was originally a defensive measure. When a player had possession of the ball and was so closely guarded that he could not pass it to one of his team mates, the only thing that he could do was to lose possession of the ball voluntarily in such a way that he might possibly recover it. He did this by rolling or bouncing the ball on the floor. This rolling or bouncing was the start of our present-day dribble. It took only a short time for the players to realize that by bouncing the ball on the floor and catching it, they could control it to some extent. The rapidity of the spread and development of the dribble was astonishing. As early as 1896, one style of game was known as the dribble game. Yale was often referred to as playing this type of game.

Very early, the double dribble was recognized. It was not known by that name, but in 1898 a clause in the rules stated that, during the dribble, a player could not touch the ball with both hands more than once. There was no limitation on the number of times that he might bounce it with one hand, however. The following year it was recognized that the dribbler could use alternate hands in bouncing the ball.

In 1901 there was a rule which stated that a player could not dribble the ball and then shoot for goal. This rule was in force in the collegiate rules until 1908, when the dribbler was again allowed to shoot for the basket.

Another type of dribble that has been little used

in the game is the overhead dribble. At first there was no limitation as to the number of times that the ball could be batted in the air, and it was not uncommon to see a player running down the floor, juggling the ball a few inches above his hand. This so closely approached running with the ball that a rule was inserted saying that the ball must be batted higher than the player' head. At the present time, a clause in the rules states that the ball may be batted in the air only once.

While the present-day dribble comes under the same restrictions that were early set down, there is a great difference in the execution of the play. To see a player take the ball and, while bouncing it on the floor, weave his way in and out through a group of players until, with a final dash, he rises high in the air and sinks the ball for a basket always thrills the crowd.

There is no doubt that the dribble as played today is wonderful to watch, but there is one objection that at the present time is serious. The officials are prone to favor the dribbler and to call fouls on anyone getting in his way. It is my opinion, and the rules plainly state it so, that the burden of personal contact comes on the dribbler. Unless this rule is enforced, there is little doubt that the dribble is due for some legislation.

2. *The Pivot.* Closely allied with the dribble is the pivot. In the early stages of the game it was not so fully developed as it is today, but a player could turn around while he was in possession of the ball as long as he did not advance. In 1893, the guide specifically stated that a man should not be considered as traveling if he turned around on the spot.

The pivot, as it is used today, has been greatly developed and is a valuable factor in the player's keeping the ball. It forms the basis of a great many plays. A few years ago there was a style of basketball that was known as the pivot-pass game. In this game, great stress was placed on the low pivot driving style. Today it is one of the important factors in the pivot-post play.

3. *The Out-of-Bounds Play.* Although basketball was supposed to eliminate the roughness of football, there was in the early period of the game one play that sometimes closely approached football tactics. The early rules stated that when a ball went out of bounds, the player who first touched it was entitled to throw it in without interference. It is easy to imagine the results of such a rule when the winning of the game became the important aim. It was not uncommon to see a player who was anxious to secure the ball make a football dive for it, regardless of whether he went into the apparatus that was stored around the gym or into the spectators in the bleachers. Lloyd Ware, one of the boys who played on an early team of mine, takes great pleasure, when in a jovial mood, in exhibiting a scar that he got when he dived for the ball and came into contact with the sharp corner of a radiator.

One other incident that I remember distinctly was a game played in a gymnasium with a balcony. Early in the first half, the ball went into the gallery, and immediately the players from one team scrambled for the narrow stairway, crowding it so that they could make little speed. Two of the players on the other team boosted one of their mates up until he could catch the lower part of the balcony, swing himself up, and regain the out-of-bounds ball.

An early rule allowed the ball to be thrown in by the player first holding it. As the rule failed to designate just what was meant by holding, many of the players felt that if they could take the ball away from someone who already had it, they would be entitled to throw it in. During that year there were so many fights that the rules committee returned to the original wording of the rule: that the ball belonged to the player first touching it.

Not until 1913 was the rule changed to state that when the ball went out of bounds, an opponent of the player who caused it to go out should put it in play. This practice led to some delay, and the following year the rule was changed to give the ball to the nearest opponent. There is little doubt that the change made at that time eliminated one of the really rough spots of the game. Today there is little confusion when the ball goes out of bounds, and it is usually returned without delay.

The Penalties

Another phase of the game that is interesting is the change that has taken place in the number and kinds of penalties. More fouls are listed today than in earlier years. The increase may be explained by the fact that many players and coaches realized that anything not forbidden in the rules was permissible. Many attempted new practices in the hope that they could gain some advantage over the opposing team. To check this tendency, it has been necessary for the rules body to legislate from time to time against certain practices that were deemed detrimental to the game.

From the first there has been a distinction between the technical and the personal fouls, although they were not known by these terms. It was plainly stated in the first printed rules that a foul committed against another person carried a certain type of penalty, whereas all other fouls carried a different penalty. The personal foul has always been considered the more serious and has consequently carried the heavier penalty.

A history of the penalties is interesting and distinctly shows how the various difficulties have been met.

At first there were only two penalties. The first time a player committed a personal foul he was warned by the referee and the violation was marked against him. The second personal foul disqualified the man until the next basket had been made. As there were nine men on a side, this penalty was not so serious as it would be today. After a basket had been made, the penalized man could enter the game and was entitled to two more fouls before he again would be disqualified.

One clause was inserted in the rules in an effort to protect a clean team from another that used rough tactics. The clause read that if three fouls were committed by one team without the other team having committed a foul, the team that was fouled should receive one point. This was rather a serious penalty, as a field goal at that time only counted one point.

Realizing that this penalty was too severe, the value of a field goal was changed from one to three points, and each foul committed against a team counted one point. Whether these fouls were technical or personal, they carried the same penalty.

The next change allowed the team that had been fouled to try for the basket from a line twenty feet from the goal. If this try was successful, the goal counted the same as one made from the field. At this same time, any person who committed two personal fouls in the same game was disqualified for the remainder of that game. If this player was disqualified from two games, he was ineligible to play for the remainder of the season. In 1895, the free-throw line was moved up to fifteen feet, and the goals from the free-throw line were counted the same as the goals from the field. In the following year, the points were changed to two for a field goal and one for a foul. The distance of the free-throw line and the value of the baskets have remained the same up to the present time.

A quotation from the rules for 1897 shows the extreme penalties meted out to the players in the early stages of the game.

> The referee may for the first offense, and shall for the second, disqualify the offender for that game and for such further period as the committee in charge of that league shall determine; except that disqualification for striking, hacking, or kicking shall be for one year without appeal.

Until 1908, the referee had the power to disqualify a man for repeated fouls. In that year, the rules stated that the player who committed five personal fouls should be disqualified for the remainder of that game. Two years later, the disqualifying number of fouls was reduced to four and has remained at that point ever since.

When the free throw was introduced, it was with the idea that many of the shots would be missed and the value of a foul would depend on the skill of the team at throwing goals; accordingly, some member of the team was designated to make the free throw. This player soon became so expert that he could throw the ball into the basket a large percentage of the time; this meant that a foul was practically as good as a goal, and led to the rule that the free throw should be made by the player against whom the foul had been made. This change was excellent, as each member of the team developed skill in this part of the game.

At the present time, there are three types of penalties: the violation that causes the violating team to lose the ball to their opponents at the nearest point on the side line; a technical foul, which allows a free throw but carries no disqualification; and the personal foul, four of which will disqualify a player for the remainder of the game.

There is considerable discussion at the present time as to the comparative value of a field goal and a foul goal. I have often overhead some spectator express the opinion that a game was won by free throws. I have always taken the attitude that the game was lost by fouls. Personally, I believe that any tendency toward lessening the penalty of a foul would be a serious mistake.

The Team

One question that seems to be of common interest to everyone is, "When was the number of players reduced to five?"

When the game was first started, it was with the idea that it should accommodate a number of people; it was the practice, especially when the game was used for recreation after a class, to divide the class into two groups, regardless of the number, and allow them to play.

Ed Hitchcock, Jr., the physical director at Cornell, had a class of about one hundred students. Following our idea, he divided this class into two teams and threw up the ball for a game. The result was that when the ball went to one end of the gym, all of the players would rush after it. Someone would get his hands on the ball and would return it to the other end of the gym, and back across the floor would dash those one hundred students. On the second day, Hitchcock decided that this plan would not do, as there was grave danger of serious damage to the building. He decided that fifty men on a side were too many for basketball.

In 1893, the first step toward setting a definite number of players was taken. It was agreed that when the game was played for sport, any number might take part, but for match games there should be a definite number of men. Five men were suggested for small gymnasiums, and nine men for the larger ones. In 1894, the rules set the number of men on a team at five when the playing space was less than eighteen hundred square feet, at seven when it was between eighteen hundred and thirty-six hundred square feet, and at nine when the floor was larger. In 1895, the number was fixed at five, unless otherwise mutually agreed upon. It was definitely settled in 1897 that a basketball team should consist of five men.

The Officials

From the beginning, the success of basketball has been largely dependent upon the officials, and to-day we are putting much stress on the selection and development of competent and efficient men for this work.

In the early days of the game, the officials were subjected to such indignities and abuse that it is hard for us to realize the conditions under which they worked. The crowds were so partial that they often resorted to violence in an effort to help their team.

I remember talking to an official named Fields about these conditions. He told me that whenever he refereed a basketball game, he was very careful to see that the window in the room where he dressed was left unlatched, in order that immediately after the game he could, if necessary, grab his clothes and leave unnoticed. Today the officials mix freely not only with the crowd but also with the players.

At first there were two officials, a referee and an umpire. The referee had control of the ball and made all decisions in connection with this part of the play, but called no fouls. The umpire had control of the men and called all fouls. It was found that the umpire as well as the referee followed the ball and caught only the fouls that were made around it. Under these conditions, the players in the back court could do as they pleased. A second umpire was introduced, whose duty it was to watch the backcourt, although he had the privilege of calling any fouls that he saw.

The next step was to return to the single umpire

and to give the referee power to call those fouls that were committed near the ball. Under these conditions, the umpire had a much better opportunity to watch the backcourt. The power of calling fouls has been gradually extended so that the referee may call fouls in any part of the court.

It was found that the expense of two disinterested officials was sometimes burdensome, and it became a practice to import the referee and use a local man for the umpire. I have often seen the local umpire undo all the work of a competent referee.

After several years of experience, the schools found that there were few officials who could handle a game alone successfully; most institutions felt that it was better to pay two disinterested officials than it was to economize and sacrifice the game. There was some attempt during the depression to return to one official, but this met with little favor.

I have had many peculiar experiences in officiating. Some of them were more comic than serious. One incident that I have often laughed about occurred while I was visiting my son in Sioux City, Iowa. One morning I dropped into the Morningside College gym and found a pick-up basketball game in progress. The boys were in need of a referee for the game, and one of the players glanced over and suggested that they get me to act in this capacity. Another of the boys looked at me and remarked,

"Huh! Come on! That old duffer never saw a game of basketball."

That evening I spoke at a banquet, and among the group were three of the boys who had played that morning. When the banquet was finished, the big fellow who had made the remark came up and shook hands. He asked me if I had been in the gym that day, and I told him that I had. A red glow came over his face as he said:

"Well, after all, I guess you were refereeing basketball games before I was born."

The Skill of the Players

In the early part of this chapter I made the statement that the greatest change in basketball has taken place in the skill with which the game is played. Beginning with no experience, each generation that has played basketball has passed on some new developments to the next. The technique and expertness with which the game is now played are indeed wonderful to me.

The scores will give some idea as to the development in skill. At first it was not uncommon to have a final score of three to four, and in several games the score was one to nothing. There were times when two teams would play an entire half without either team scoring. Today there are teams that, throughout the season, have scored a point for every minute of play.

Practice may be given much of the credit for the scores that we have at the present time, and it is not uncommon to see from one to ten boys shooting baskets from different positions on the floor. This basket shooting is not a game, but merely a series of attempts to throw the ball into the basket.

I remember walking across the gym floor one day and seeing a boy toss the ball toward the basket, recover it, and toss it again. An hour later, as I came back through the gym, the same boy was still at his play. For some time I had been trying to discover what there was about goal throwing that would keep a boy at it for an hour. I stopped and asked him why he was practicing so long. The boy answered that he did not know, but that he just liked to see if he could make a basket every time he threw the ball.

It is little wonder that with practice of this kind, along with the other fundamentals that have been passed down, the players of today are much more expert than those who first played the game.

The Ten-Second Rule

I should like to discuss at some length one change that has been made in the rules. Before doing so, however, I should like to make it clear that I am interested in the game of basketball from the standpoint of the players and the spectators rather than from the standpoint of the highly specialized coaches.

In 1901 there was introduced into basketball a style of play called the five-man defense. This defense was a direct effort to meet a condition in which all five men, on gaining possession of the ball, rushed down the floor to try to score. This type of offense was first played on the Pacific Coast. Before this time, the men had been more or less scattered, and the game was comparatively open. With the concentration of the offense, the defensive men opposed it by concentration near their own goal.

Under these conditions, both the defense and the offense became so specialized that a system of scoring plays and a set defense came into vogue. The development of these systems in the last few years has presented a vital problem in basketball.

The set defense became harder and harder to penetrate, and the offense became more and more reluctant to crash into those five closely grouped players. This reluctance was especially shown by teams that were in the lead and who already had the game won. After all, why should these men who had already shown their superiority attempt to increase their score when the other team was not interested enough to come out and attempt to get the ball? It was seldom that a team could score, unless it had possession of the ball.

Some time after the five-man defense was introduced to the game, the matter of stalling became one of grave concern. The crowds were not attending the games as they had, and the players were not so enthusiastic as they had been. Something had to be done. At this point, a few men who were exponents of the five-man defense made a great cry about the harm of stalling. Through newspaper propaganda, the spectators were led to believe that the team in possession of the ball was doing the stalling, and for some time when the offensive team refused to enter a closely set defense, the crowd would boo and accuse them of stalling.

It is my contention, and that of many coaches with whom I have talked, that when this condition occurs, the blame should be placed on the team that does not attempt to get the ball.

In 1901, someone wrote to George T. Hepbron, editor of the guide for that year and still a member of the rules committee, and asked this question:

> Is there any rule, stated or implied, against holding the ball for any length of time within bounds?

Hepbron's answer follows:

> There is no rule stated or implied against holding the ball for any length of time within bounds. The opponent of the man with the ball generally decides how long he shall hold it. I cannot understand how any man can hold the ball for any length of time without another player interfering and attempting to get it. However, if there is such a case, rule 11, section 38, can be applied to it. [This rule has to do with intentional delay of the game. Naturally, the ball may not be held more than ten seconds in the backcourt.]

The slogan of basketball has always been "Play the ball and not the man," and for many years it has been a common thing through certain sections of the country to hear E. C. Quigley blow his whistle and in a stentorian voice say, "You can't do that! Play the ball, not the man."

In the 1931 basketball guide there is an article entitled "For the Sake of the Game," written by Dr. F. C. Allen, one of the most successful basketball coaches in the country. In this article, Doctor Allen, speaking of his basketball team from the Haskell Institute, said:

Earlier in the year I had impressed upon the Indians the fact that they were playing with that ball. It was their ball—for them to get it. They had to get it to play with it.

These statements clearly indicate that in order to play the game of basketball, one must at least try to gain possession of the ball.

When the five-man defense introduced the stalling game in which one team refused to make an attempt to get the ball, the condition became so serious that it was agreed that something must be done. Some teams, when on the defense, had clustered around the basket and remained in this position for nineteen minutes, making no advance toward the ball. Under these conditions, the people were forced to sit in their seats and watch ten men on the floor doing nothing. A great many people did not care to pay to see two teams at opposite ends of the floor looking at each other.

At a meeting of the coaches in 1932, this subject was discussed. It was agreed by most of the coaches that they should eliminate this hazard to the popularity of the game. A number of suggestions was considered.

I was not present at this meeting, but I had been studying this objectionable feature for some time and had come to the conclusion that there were three ways in which the evil might be remedied. I made the following suggestions to the rules committee:

1. Any team that retreated under the basket and refused to make an attempt to get the ball for thirty seconds should be penalized by giving the other side a free throw. [This was simply putting into effect the statement that had been made by Hepbron and which for thirty years had been overlooked by the officials.]

2. Any basket that was shot from outside of the defensive players should count four points.

3. That not more than three defensive players be allowed in the defensive half of the court while the ball was in the other half.

All three of these suggestions clearly put the burden of stalling on the defensive team.

At the coaches' meeting, after some discussion, it was decided to recommend a rule that would force the offensive team to take the ball to the defensive team, instead of getting them out of their close formation.

When this rule was first demonstrated, I was present at the exhibition game and was asked to make some comment on the rule. I told the men in charge that I disagreed with them, but they still insisted. When I was called on to speak, I said that I had several objections to the adoption of the rule.

First of all, it would not stop stalling. My contention has been proved again and again since that time, as it was by one incident that occurred in the 1934 National Tournament. The Stage Liners took the ball into the front court and held it for twelve minutes without an attempt to make a basket. During this time the ball was not held by one man, but was passed from man to man. By actual count, there were three hundred forty-three passes without an attempt to make a goal. There have been many other examples that plainly show that stalling has not been stopped by the adoption of the ten-second rule.

My second objection was that it necessarily crowded all of the men into one half of the court. This crowding could not help but make for roughness, and an increase in the number of fouls was inevitable. The coaches are faced today with the problem of finding some way to spread the teams. Three suggestions that have been made are to raise the goal to twelve feet, to bring the goal five feet into the field, and to enlarge the basket. All of these suggestions have as an objective the spreading of the defense.

The third objection that I made was that this

rule mechanized the game, taking it largely out of the hands of the players and giving it to the coaches. When an offensive team slowly went down the floor toward a set defense, there was little chance but that those players would try to execute some play in which they had been thoroughly drilled. These players were not allowed to think for themelves, but were supposed to do one certain thing. Players had often been pulled out of a game by the coach, because they wished to play ball and violated some order that the coach had given. An incident of this kind came when the star player on a team left the defense to rush out and get the ball. He was successful in his attempt, and taking the other team by surprise, dribbled down the floor and made a beautiful goal. The crowd wildly acclaimed this feat, but the boy was removed from the game for failure to follow exactly the instructions of the coach. The practice is more common in the high schools today than in universities, but both groups are afflicted with this evil.

It was to practices like these that I objected. Why should the play of a group of young men be entirely spoiled to further the ambitions of some coach?

I should like to say in regard to stalling, "Throw the blame on the team that refuses to play the ball.

Give the boys a chance to use their own initiative. Make use of the space that we have at the present time on our basketball floors, rather than jam ten men into a court that is little larger than the one on which basketball started."

The Center Jump

Since the elimination of the center jump except at the start of each half and following a "double foul," there has been considerable controversy. The center jump was originally designed to give each team an equal chance to get the ball, and the team with the better jumper had the advantage. There was never any objection to a team that had an exceptional jumper and could secure the tip every time; but today there is an objection to the team that gains this same advantage by the use of a very tall man.

Height is not the only factor that can be used in jumping for the ball; ability to jump and judgment as to when to jump are as important as height. If the officials would toss the ball higher in the air and at varying heights, much of the advantage of the tall man would be lost.

In a class in kinesiology, the question of judgment versus height was brought up. In order to satisfy the members of the class, two basketball players

were selected, one four inches taller than the other.
A basketball was obtained, and we went out on the
gymnasium floor. I tossed the ball between them,
each time just above the point which the taller man
could reach, and without exception the taller man
gained the tip. Next I tossed the ball consider-
ably higher, and under these conditions the shorter
man was able to gain the tip an equal number of
times. The next step was to toss the ball high and
at different heights each time, and under these
conditions the shorter man had a decided advantage in the number of tips received. I was convinced that this high toss at varying heights would
largely overcome the advantage gained by height
alone.

Personally, I feel that the center jump is to
basketball what the kick-off is to football. To
award the ball to a team after a goal is scored takes
away much of the thrill that is present in an opening play. A crowd does not rise to its feet in excitement at the start of a play when the ball is simply
given to a team.

CHAPTER V

DEVELOPMENT OF BASKET-BALL EQUIPMENT

A FEW years ago I was asked by a committee at a physical education convention to reproduce the first basketball game. At first I thought that this would be comparatively easy, and I began to visualize the material for an accurate reproduction.

As I recalled that first game, I began to realize that the job would not be so easy as I had at first thought. The old gymnasium at Springfield would be hard to reproduce under the present conditions. I remembered the dim lights that were set in the ceiling, the great mass of apparatus that was shoved into the corners, the walls lined with clubs, dumbbells, and wands, and the gallery that ran completely the length of the floor. The more I thought of reproducing these conditions, the more dubious I became.

It would be comparatively easy to obtain a couple of peach baskets and a soccer ball for the game, and this much I would not need to worry about.

The next difficulty that presented itself was to find eighteen players. To be truly representative of that first group, there should be some with walrus mustaches and some with full beards, the others looking comparatively modern. None of them should ever have seen a basketball game. This was a problem that would be hard to solve. I might be able, in a city of one hundred thousand, to find eighteen young men with the proper facial adornment. I felt sure that I could find eighteen men who had never seen a basketball game, but to find the combination was another matter. After thinking the matter over, I decided that the whole show would be a case of acting and that it would be impossible for any group of young men who had ever handled a basketball to approach the confusion and awkwardness of that first team without a great deal of coaching.

Writing to the committee, I explained to them that unless they could find the men required, I did not feel that I had the time to coach a group so that it could give an authentic idea of the first game. Realizing the difficulties, the committee decided to omit this part of the program.

I have had many requests for a description of this first game, in order that it might be reproduced. Even since starting to write this chapter, I have had such a request from a school in Wisconsin. A description of some of the changes that have taken place in basketball equipment in the past forty years may, therefore, be entertaining.

The Uniforms

For the first few years, the basketball uniform was any suit that was used in the gymnasium. Some of the teams used the long trousers and short-sleeved jerseys, others used track suits, and some even played in the clothes that they used on the football field.

The first basketball outfit was listed in the Spalding catalogue in 1901, and the advertisements for these suits would today seem ridiculous. There were three types of pants suggested as being correct for the game. There were the knee length padded pants that were almost exactly like those used on the football field, and the short padded pants that, except for length, resembled those of the present day. Last were the knee-length jersey tights. Any of these pants appearing on the floor today would cause hoots of amazement.

The rest of the equipment was not so striking. It is true that the quarter length sleeves were used, but sleeveless shirts were also suggested.

The first suction sole basketball shoes were advertised by the Spalding Company in 1903. These were guaranteed not to slip even on a dancing floor. There was also a statement in the advertisement that the team equipped with these suction soled shoes possessed a decided advantage over the team that did not have them.

The Ball

Probably the piece of equipment that has had fewest changes is the ball. For the first two years it was an ordinary Association (soccer) football, and it was not until 1894 that there was any such thing as a basketball. In this year a larger ball was adopted as the official ball for the game. This ball was made by the Overman Wheel Company, who were manufacturers of bicycles at Chicopee Falls, Massachusetts. It is surprising how little change has taken place since that time.

In 1894 the rule read that the ball should be not less than thirty inches nor more than thirty-two in circumference. The 1933 rules listed the same specifications. There was some change in the 1934 rules, but it was negligible. The spherical shape of the ball is shown by the rule that was inserted in the Guide of 1898. This rule states that the ball shall not vary more than a quarter of an inch in any diameter.

In 1898 the weight of the ball was established at a minimum of eighteen ounces and a maximum of twenty ounces. This remained the official weight until 1909, when the manufacturers complained that they could not make a ball of the required weight that would have the required lasting qualities. The weight was then increased to a minimum of twenty and a maximum of twenty-two ounces. This weight still remains.

The Goal

The goals, as has been stated many times, were originally peach baskets. These were so frail that they would last only a short time. In 1892, Lew Allen of Hartford, Connecticut, conceived the idea of making cylindrical baskets of heavy woven wire. The peach baskets that had been used were larger at the top than at the bottom. When they were nailed to a flat surface, the outer edge of the basket was somewhat lower than the edge against the support. This condition was corrected by the cylindrical wire baskets.

In 1893, the Narragansett Machine Company of Providence, Rhode Island, manufactured a basket that was very similar to the one that is in use today. It was made of an iron rim and a cord basket.

It was stated in the rules at first that the ball must stay in the basket in order to count as a goal; and since the basket was ten feet from the ground, there had to be some way of getting the ball out. When the goal was fastened to the gallery, the ball was easily retrieved by anyone who could reach over the balcony rail. When the basket was against the wall, however, it was sometimes necessary to use a ladder to get the ball. Later we made a practice of drilling a hole in the bottom of the peach baskets in order that a wand might be inserted from below and the ball might be punched out in this manner. Since the pole was often missing, we had to resort to many other devices. On account of the inexperience of the players, fortunately, the goals were few and far between.

The Narragansett, realizing our difficulties, constructed a goal with the net entirely closed. When a goal was made, the ball stayed in the basket. To get the ball out of this basket, an ingenious device was installed. A chain was fastened to the bottom of the net and passed over a pulley on the brace that fastened the basket to the support. To empty the basket, the referee pulled the handle of the chain and the ball rolled out.

As the skill of the players increased, they demanded that the equipment be exact, and especially that the goals be horizontal. To meet these demands, a basket was constructed in which the braces, instead of being welded, were screwed into the rims. This allowed the rims of the goal to be properly adjusted.

It is only in comparatively recent years that the goal has been made without braces and the nets have been opened at the lower end to allow the ball to pass through. Today, a clause in the rules states that the ball shall be momentarily checked as it passes through the net. This rule is frequently neglected; and the ball passes through the net so quickly that the spectators are in doubt as to whether a goal has been made or missed.

The Backboards

The backboards are really the only accessory of the game that are accidental in their origin. Had it not been for the overzealous spectators who gladly used any means to help their team win, the backboard might not be in use today.

When the game began to attract crowds, the only available space for them was in the gallery. As the baskets were nailed to the lower edge of the balcony, it was easy for a person to thrust his hand suddenly through the rail and deflect the ball enough to make it enter or miss the goal, as he desired.

I can distinctly remember one boy about fifteen years old who used to come into the balcony and take a place directly behind the basket. He came early in order that he might always get this seat. He patiently waited an opportunity to help his team by darting his hand through the rail at the proper time to help the ball into the basket.

To do away with this practice, the following year a clause was entered in the rules, which stated that the goal must be protected from the spectators by a screen at least six feet on each side of the goal and at least six feet high. In 1895, the rules stated that there should be a backstop made of screen or other solid material and the size, six feet by four feet, was definitely settled at that time. This is the size of the regulation backboard today.*

When the backboard was made of wood, it interfered with the view of the spectators who were seated behind the goal. This interference came at the most interesting time, when the ball was shot for the basket. To allow the spectators to see the goal, most of the backboards were made of heavy screen.

* A "fan"-shaped board fifty-four inches by thirty-five inches may also be used.

TIME MARCHES ON—1893
To Release the Ball, You Merely Pull the Chain

BASKET.

O

Home.

L. Forward.   R. Forward   Forwards.

. . . .

Center.

L. Center.   R. Center.   Center Men.

. . . .

L. Back.   R. Back.   Backs.

Goal Keeper.

O

BASKET.

Diagram of Basket Ball—position of players.

10

POSITIONS OF THE PLAYERS
From the Second Edition of the Rules Book, 1893

There were several objections to these screen backboards, however. A visiting team was under a distinct handicap. If the screen was comparatively loose, it would have a certain amount of "give," and the rebound would be slight.

Another objection to the screen was that after some play, and sometimes by scientific manipulation, the screen would become grooved, and the home team, knowing these peculiarities, would have a decided advantage. These facts led to the introduction of the wooden backboards.

In 1909, plate glass backboards were introduced, in order that the spectators behind the goals might see the ball as it was thrown for the basket. Many of the universities and larger institutions used these backboards for several years. There were, however, some objections. The teams that did not have the glass backboards found themselves at a disadvantage when required to play on a court which was equipped with them.

The carom shot was not the same on the glass as it was on the wooden backboard; for the players who were shooting, on looking at the basket, found it suspended without a background. This circumstance made it difficult for a team that had been practicing on the wooden equipment.

When, in 1916, the rules read that the backboards must be painted white, the plate glass backs were considered to be of no further value and were discontinued. However, they are extremely popular today.

The Court

It would be hard for us today to visualize a basketball court with an imaginary boundary line; but so far as the rules were concerned, this was the condition for the first two years of the game.

In 1894, the rules specified that there must be a well-defined line around the playing area at least three feet from the wall or fence. The boundary line naturally followed the contour of the gymnasium walls, which in many cases had projections to accommodate stairways or offices. Many courts were of irregular shape, frequently being wider at one end than at the other. The team that played on the narrow end was therefore handicapped.

In 1903, a clause was inserted in the rules stating that the boundary lines must be straight. Later the rules specifically stated that the court must be a rectangle.

As the game was originally designed to be played on any court, there was no regulation size, the only stipulation being that the larger the court, the greater the number of players. In 1896, when the team was definitely cut to five men, the rules contained a provision that the court should not exceed thirty-five hundred square feet of playing space. This size court was official until 1908, when the maximum court was set as ninety feet long and fifty-five feet wide. The width of the court was reduced to fifty feet in 1915.

In 1917, E. C. Quigley, who is in reality the dean of basketball officials, made a suggestion to the rules committee that proved to be of great value. For years "Quig," in his capacity as an official, had raced from one end of gymnasiums to the other. One of his greatest difficulties was to determine whether a man who was shooting for a basket under his goal, was in or out of bounds. The goal at that time was directly over the end line, and in the confusion that often occurred under the basket, it was almost impossible to determine just who was in and who was out of bounds. If the basket was made while the player had his foot on the line, it was invalid; this point was the cause of many heated disputes.

At St. Mary's College, Kansas, Quigley tried an experiment that led to his suggestion. He drew the arc of a circle under the basket and two feet beyond the end line; this area was considered in bounds. After a year's experiment, Quigley found that this change not only did away with much of the indecision but also helped the game, as it allowed more space under the basket.

The rules committee saw the value of Quigley's suggestion, and in 1917 they introduced the end zone, the radius of which was seventeen feet, with its center on the free throw line. This end zone was so successful that the following year the extension went entirely across the court. At first the end zones were not included in the court, but in 1933 they became recognized as part of the playing field. The addition of these end zones has increased the length of the court until today the maximum official court is ninety-four by fifty feet.

In 1922, a goal zone line was added to the floor markings. This line was simply an extension of the free-throw line to meet the side lines. It was felt that a foul committed in this area by a defensive player should be more severely dealt with than one committed on some other part of the floor. The rules for that year stated that a foul committed by a defensive player in this territory should carry the penalty of two free throws instead of one. This goal zone was short-lived, and in 1925 it was dropped from the guide.

In 1932, a line across the center of the floor was introduced. This line divided the field into two courts called the front and the back court, according to the team in possession of the ball. Today the use of this line is causing much controversy.

CHAPTER VI

CHANGES IN THE RULES BODY

THERE is one group of men who, because of their interest in basketball, have given time and care to the development of the game. They have had at heart the interest of the great mass of people who are playing. I consider that the men who have spent their time in studying, developing, and clarifying the rules of basketball should receive adequate recognition for their efforts. I sincerely hope that these men realize how much their work has meant to the game.

That basketball should spread as it has was beyond our wildest imagination; and for the first two years, the changes that were made and the editing of the rules fell entirely on my shoulders. The first two guides were printed by the Triangle Publishing Company, a school organization, which was given largely to publishing articles and books for the Y.M.C.A. These two guides were vest-pocket editions, giving simply the aims and the rules of the game.

In 1894, Dr. Gulick made the suggestion that we should clarify and expand the rules. There were so many questions and requests for details of the game that to answer these was more than any one man could handle. We hoped that, by changing the make-up of the guide, the game would be clearer to those who had taken it up from the book alone.

We spent many hours in revising and rewording the previous guides and felt that the guide for that year would clear up many of the questions that had been sent in the year before.

In the summer of 1895 I left Sprinfigeld to accept a position as head of the physical education department in the Y.M.C.A. in Denver, Colorado. As this position took me away from what was then the center of basketball, Dr. Gulick took over the responsibility of editing the rules. For two years the Doctor assumed this task, but at the end of that time he realized that help was needed.

Basketball had spread so rapidly that one or two men could not meet the problems that arose. The fact that the game belonged to the public made us realize that an organization was necessary to develop the game and to make changes in the rules.

Doctor Gulick decided that a committee should be formed, but at this early stage of the game he hesitated to call a group of men together from different parts of the country. Instead, he sent questionnaires throughout the United States. Those receiving the questionnaires were asked to offer suggestions for changes in the rules; it was in this manner that Dr. Gulick obtained much of the sentiment from different sections of the country. The answers and suggestions that were received formed the basis for the changes made in the rules the following year.

The first basketball rules committee was called the Basketball Co-Operating Committee, and its members were the men who had answered Dr. Gulick's questionnaire. Many of the men who were on this first committee are still alive and are vitally interested in basketball.

Until the Co-Operating Committee came into existence, the making and developing of the rules had been entirely in the hands of the Y.M.C.A. This situation had not been satisfactory, as there were so many basketball organizations over which the Y.M.C.A. had no control. There was a need of centralized authority to stabilize the game.

Realizing its inability to control the game, the Y.M.C.A. asked the Amateur Athletic Union to assume the responsibility. Many teams were unable to conform to the standards of the A.A.U.

Basketball teams, therefore, were divided into three groups: first, the amateur teams that were registered with the A.A.U.; second, the teams which were amateurs but were not registered; and third, the distinctly professional teams. The division of the teams caused much confusion, and some antagonism developed toward the A.A.U. Among the teams that were registered, the organization assumed a strict attitude, not allowing any of its members to compete with outside teams and even demanding that registered teams obtain sanction from headquarters before playing a game.

The teams that were not registered with the A.A.U. were under no such restrictions and played among themselves, but were unable to play teams in the A.A.U. The professional teams gradually drew away from the amateur groups and formed leagues. In 1901, they began to edit and print their own set of rules, known as the *Reach Official Basketball Guide*. The professionals used this guide until 1927, when they adopted the uniform rules and made a few changes that they felt necessary.

When the A.A.U. first assumed control of basketball there was little doubt that it would eventually have most of the teams in the country registered in its organization. The number of teams that did register, however, was in the vast minority. This left the great majority of the teams outside the jurisdiction of the A.A.U., and it lost its control.

In 1905, a group of men representing several of the colleges felt that, since the game had been so widely adopted by the universities, they themselves should publish the rules. Accordingly, representatives from seven schools (Yale, Pennsylvania, Columbia, Harvard, Princeton, Cornell, and Minnesota) formulated a set of rules that was published by the Spalding Company and called the *Official Collegiate Basketball Guide*. A quotation from the first guide published by this group clearly indicates their attitude:

> Since basketball has been universally accepted by colleges as a permanent winter sport, there has been expressed from time to time demands that the making of the rules should be placed in the hands of the colleges themselves. This feeling emanated from no dissatisfaction with the existing rules but rather from the desire to secure uniform interpretation and to provide an easily accessible means for effecting changes which at any time should be considered necessary.

Although the colleges said that they were not dissatisfied with the official rules, they objected to certain sections. These sections were concerned largely with registration and the necessity of obtaining the sanction from the A.A.U. for their games, as well as the statements that dealt with the conduct of the players. A statement from the first collegiate guide says:

> Nothing concerning the eligibility or personal conduct of the players has been embodied in the rules.

The split in the amateur ranks was destined to last for some years. The A.A.U. continued to publish one set of rules, and the colleges published another.

In 1908, the National Collegiate Athletic Association decided that since the collegiate rules had been such a success, it would publish them. The men who had originally formulated the collegiate rules were all retained on the new committee. The decision of the N.C.A.A. materially strengthened the collegiate rules, and they were almost universally adopted by the colleges.

It was not until 1915 that the Y.M.C.A., realizing the disadvantage of having two sets of rules, went to the college group to discuss combining the two sets. This conference resulted in an agreement by these two organizations, and the A.A.U. accepted the invitation to join. The merging of these three groups resulted in the Joint Basketball Committee, which today is in charge of the basketball rules.

It was agreed at this first meeting that each organization would be represented, and in order that no discrimination be shown, names of the different organizations were to be rotated in the guides.

Though the personnel of the committee has changed many times and the number of representatives from the different organizations has varied, the three original organizations are still represented. Three others have since been added: the Chartered Board of Officials in 1927, and the National Federation of State High School Athletic Associations and the Canadian Amateur Basketball Association in 1929.

In 1933, the *Guide* failed to register the Chartered Board of Officials as a member of the Joint Committee, but I was informed that this body is still affiliated with the rules committee.

It is only natural that from the first I have followed the changes made in the rules, and even while I was not on the committee in charge, I was actively interested.

In 1909, when the N.C.A.A. took over the editing of the collegiate rules, I was appointed as a member of this committee and served until I left for France in 1917. On my return I was inactive on the committee until 1923, when I was appointed by the

N.C.A.A. as an honorary member for life; in the following year I was designated as honorary chairman of the rules committee for life.

It has always been a pleasure to be able to work with the committee, to discuss the problems that arose, and in some small measure to help keep the game for that great mass of American youth.

ORGANIZATION OF THE RULES GOVERNING BODY *

1892 Young Men's Christian Association

1896 Young Men's Christian Association
Amateur Athletic Union

1915 Young Men's Christian Association
Amateur Athletic Union
National Collegiate Athletic Association

1927 Young Men's Christian Association
Amateur Athletic Union
National Collegiate Athletic Association
Chartered Board of Officials

1929 Young Men's Christian Association
Amateur Athletic Union
National Collegiate Athletic Association
Chartered Board of Officials
National Federation of State High School Athletic
Associations
Canadian Amateur Basketball Association

1933 Young Men's Christian Association
Amateur Athletic Union
National Collegiate Athletic Association
National Federation of State High School Athletic
Associations
Canadian Amateur Basketball Association

* This chart indicates the length of time that the organizations have
been in the rules committee and the growth from the one organization
to the present quota of five.

CHAPTER VII

THE SPREAD OF THE GAME
IN THE UNITED STATES

SEVERAL years ago, as I was returning from a summer trip in Colorado, I came by the way of the so-called world's highest bridge, spanning the Royal Gorge a few miles above Canyon City, Colo. At the south end of the bridge we came upon the deserted camp of the men who had built the structure. There was little to tell of the number of men and boys who had spent many months playing and working on this spot. At one end of the former camp, however, there were two basketball backstops. The goals had been removed, and they stood alone against the dark pines, a mute reminder of the activity that had once been a part of the camp life.

I am sure that no man can derive more pleasure from money or power than I do from seeing a pair of basketball goals in some out of the way place— deep in the Wisconsin woods an old barrel hoop nailed to a tree, or a weather-beaten shed on the

Mexican border with a rusty iron hoop nailed to one end. These sights are constant reminders that I have in some measure accomplished the objective that I set up years ago.

Thousands of times, especially in the last few years, I have been asked whether I ever got anything out of basketball. To answer this question, I can only smile. It would be impossible for me to explain my feelings to the great mass of people who ask this question, as my pay has not been in dollars but in the satisfaction of giving something to the world that is a benefit to masses of people.

Grantland Rice once estimated that there were fifteen million people playing basketball. This number to me is inconceivable, but I do not believe that it is exaggerated. The number of boys and girls who are playing the game in our educational institutions alone will run into the millions, and these institutions are only one group of the many that are playing the game.

The spread of basketball has been both extensive and rapid. The game was introduced into the foreign countries soon after its origin, and it spread here in the United States so rapidly that I have been unable to determine accurately just when many parts of the country took up the game. There

RULES

FOR

☀ BASKET BALL ☀

BY

JAS. NAISMITH

INSTRUCTOR IN

International Y. M. C. A. Training School

SPRINGFIELD, MASS.

✿

PRESS OF
SPRINGFIELD PRINTING AND BINDING COMPANY
1892

TITLE PAGE OF THE FIRST BOOK OF RULES, 1892

THE GAME SPREADS OUT: FROM HERE—

18,000 SEE L. I. U. BEAT OREGON FIVE IN GARDEN BY 43-31

Blackbirds, in Front by 21-17 at Half, Triumph Easily in College Opener at Arena

---

CITY COLLEGE IS SET BACK

Bows to Oklahoma Aggies in Second Contest of Card by Margin of 32 to 24

By LOUIS EFFRAT

College basketball's 1940-41 debut at Madison Square Garden last night attracted a capacity turnout of 18,000 to the Eighth Avenue arena, where an intersectional double-header pitted L. I. U. against Oregon and C. C. N. Y. against the Oklahoma Aggies.

········ ···· raiser the towering
········ ·····   beaten in

Courtesy, Madison Square Garden Official Basketball Program

—TO HERE

* BASKET * BALL. *

Basket Ball is not a game intended merely for amusement, but is the attempted solution of a problem which has been pressing on physical educators. Most of the games which are played out of doors are unsuitable for indoors, and consequently whenever the season closes, the game, together with all the benefits to be derived therefrom, is dropped. It is true that some players have been accustomed to keep up a desultory kind of training but it lacked the all-round development that is so requisite, and very frequently failed to give that training for the heart and lungs which is so desirable. A number of gymnasiums have running tracks, but even then it is more or less uninteresting to run around a gallery so many times per day.

There were certain definite conditions to be met by the game which was required, and these had to be complied with before it could be pronounced satisfactory.

1st. It should be such as could be played on any kind of ground,—in a gymnasium, a large room, a small lot, a large field, whether these had uneven or smooth surface, so that no special preparation is little doubt but that there are more people playing basketball in the United States than in all the foreign countries.

The Y.M.C.A.

As the game originated in the Y.M.C.A. Training School in Springfield, Massachusetts, it was only natural that much of the early spread should come through that institution. The Y.M.C.A. was one of the few organizations interested in physical development, and the fact that most of the branches had gymnasiums was an important factor in the spread of the game through this institution.

There were two ways in which the Y.M.C.A. spread the game. The *Triangle,* the school paper, printed a description of the game and the rules in January, 1892. This paper went to the branches of the Y.M.C.A. all over the country; and as these branches were looking desperately for some activity that would interest their members, they quickly accepted the game. It was only a short time after the publication of the paper containing the rules that I received requests for details about the game. These letters came from widely scattered points, but practically all of them were from Y.M.C.A. branches. One of the first letters that I received was from George W. Ehler, of the Central Branch of the Brooklyn Y.M.C.A. In his letter of April, 1892, Mr. Ehler said that he had introduced basketball into the Brooklyn branch and that the members there were more enthusiastic about the game than one could imagine. Just how many other New York branches were playing is not known, but Mr. Ehler stated that the Brooklyn team had scheduled several games with other Y.M.C.A.'s.

While the Y.M.C.A.'s were quite generally adopting the game, there were some branches which were having trouble with it, especially in certain sections in the East. The physical directors of that time were judged by the number of members that they had in their classes. Basketball would allow only ten men on a floor that would normally accommodate fifty or sixty. This monopoly of the floor by a few caused some of the physical directors to question the value of the game, as they felt that development work for a large group was more important than a recreative game in which only a few men could participate.

Another problem that presented itself was the fact that many directors lacked experience in handling competitive sports. This lack of experience was responsible for some roughness and unsportsmanlike conduct on the part of many teams.

Philadelphia was one of the cities in which basketball became so popular that it threatened to disrupt the formal gymnastic classes that were carried on in the Association. So many teams were organized and the game was so popular that if teams were allowed to use the gymnasium, there would be little time for other work. To meet this condition, the North Branch of the Y.M.C.A. in that city refused to allow a basketball on the gymnasium floor.

On March 27, 1897, Doctor Chadwick, of the Philadelphia Y.M.C.A., published an article in which he requested that the game be dropped by the Association because of its monopoly of the floor and its evil effect on the Association's reputation and influence. As a result of this restriction on the game in the Philadelphia branches, many members withdrew and formed independent teams. These teams played among themselves, using any kind of gymnasium that could be found. Games were held in warehouses and even in dance halls supplied with goals.

These independent teams soon found that the spectators crowded the floor; and to meet this condition, the teams constructed cages that would prevent the ball from going out of bounds. The playing of basketball under these conditions was responsible for the start of the professional game; and as far as I am able to determine, Philadelphia had the first team of this type.

In spite of the fact that only a few of the Y.M.C.A. branches were having difficulty with basketball, it was decided that a study should be made to determine the attitude of the organization toward the game. M. T. J. Browne, selected to carry out this study, sent a questionnaire to some hundred of the different branches. When he compiled the results of these questionnaires, he found that a majority of the institutions felt that basketball had not only helped to hold the older members but had also increased the membership, and that it had created a greater loyalty toward the Association.

With the realization that basketball was a great help, the Y.M.C.A. turned its efforts to teaching thousands of boys all over the country to play the game. With the construction of other gymnasiums and the enlarging of their own buildings, the Association has provided ample space. Although many teams were playing in other gymnasiums, the Y.M.C.A. still managed much of the organization of leagues and tournaments. Today thousands of boys' teams all over the country are using the Association equipment and are playing and practicing in the buildings, often without any charge.

The students of the Training School also spread the game. They represented many different parts of the country, and as these men finished their courses and scattered to their respective homes or fields of work, they took the game with them. Since the school was international, not only the United States but also several of the foreign countries received the game from men who were either classmates or students of mine. France and Japan were both represented in the class of 1893. When Theis returned to Paris, he took with him the first knowledge of the new game. I have been unable to determine whether Ishakawa introduced the game into the orient when he left the University of Wisconsin and returned to his native country, but certainly he was interested, as he furnished the first sketch of a basketball game, which was printed in the 1893 guide.

Basketball owes a great deal to the Y.M.C.A., because it was first to recognize the necessity for a winter sport, it furnished the facilities and the opportunity to originate the game, and it was a means of spreading the game over the entire world, as its foreign introduction came largely through the branches of the Association in the various countries.

The A.A.U. and the Athletic Clubs

Soon after the Y.M.C.A. had accepted basketball, the athletic clubs began to take up the game. Many of these clubs were formed for the purpose of playing basketball, whereas others that were of old standing organized teams. The athletic clubs of that time were primarily for the development of sports and were interested in the promotion of athletic teams rather than social activities.

In 1897, there were fifty-eight athletic clubs that had organized basketball teams, and these teams were competing with teams from all types of institutions. Today there are a great many clubs represented at the National Basketball Tournament, and, with few exceptions, these teams are well up in the running. It has always been interesting to me to note the number of former college players listed on the various athletic club teams. Many of the members of the clubs are unable to give the time for practice during the day, and this difficulty has been largely overcome by obtaining players who have been thoroughly drilled in the fundamentals. It is not uncommon to see a whole team composed of former college players, men who need little training and who in two or three evenings a week can organize and polish their play.

I am sure that the opportunity for these young men to continue their activity after leaving college is of immense value, and much credit must be given the athletic clubs for furnishing this opportunity.

For many years the Kansas City Athletic Club sponsored a team, and several times won the National Tournament. Subsequently the Olympic Club, which came from California to compete, rated among the best in the tournament. Other clubs from both coasts were represented. It is always a pleasure to meet these men, as, without exception, I have always noticed that the highest type of sportsmanship is exhibited by the teams from the clubs.

Colleges

To the colleges all over the country, basketball owes much. There has been no other institution that has so advanced the technique and skill of the game. In return for this advancement, basketball has given to the colleges a winter sport that is recognized the world over, which is not only self-supporting but also important in the college intramural programs.

When basketball was originated, the colleges were comparatively slow to adopt the game. Some schools played very early, but it was not until about 1900 that they recognized the game as an important

part of the college sports program. One of the
reasons that the colleges did not play basketball
earlier was that the coaches and physical directors
were not familiar with the new sport. The colleges
did not really accept the game until the boys who
had learned basketball in the Y.M.C.A. and high
schools enrolled with them. Many of the college
physical directors think that the colleges introduced
basketball into the high schools, but in reality the
high schools introduced basketball into many of the
colleges.

Geneva College, in Beaver Falls, Pennsylvania,
and the University of Iowa both played basketball
in the season of 1892. Which of these two colleges
may claim the first game, I do not know. Mr.
C. O. Beamis, a Springfield boy, had gone to Geneva
College as physical director. Beamis had seen the
game played in the Training School gymnasium
while he was home on a vacation. He realized that
it might solve the need of a winter activity in his
school. I told him of the success we had and explained to him the fundamentals of the game. On
his return to Beaver Falls he started the game in
Geneva College; it is my belief, therefore, that this
college was the first to play basketball. Iowa might
have played as early as Geneva. In 1890, H. F.
Kallenberg was an instructor at the Springfield

school and left to accept a position at Iowa in 1891. When the basketball rules were published, Mr. Kallenberg obtained a set and organized a group of teams. I have corresponded with both schools, but I have not been able to learn just when either school played its first game.

Leland Stanford also played the game soon after its origin, under the direction of W. O. Black. In 1893, Mr. Black graduated from Springfield and accepted a position in the physical education department at Leland Stanford. Black had played basketball while attending school, and soon after his arrival at the California school he organized a team.

During 1894 and 1895, many of the Eastern colleges began to play basketball. They were at first handicapped because they could find so few opponents among colleges that it was hard to schedule games. Many of the early college teams were forced to play Y.M.C.A., high school, and other outside organizations; it was not uncommon to have the college teams of this period soundly trounced by some secondary school team or one that was made up of some group of younger boys.

In the winter of 1893, two teams from Springfield played an exhibition game at a physical directors' convention in the Yale gymnasium. Pearson S.

Page, the physical director at Andover, reminded me in a letter a few years ago that he had played on one of the Springfield exhibition teams. Many of these directors had never seen a basketball game, and on returning to their respective schools, began to organize teams. Dr. W. H. Anderson, of Yale, who was present at this convention, soon introduced the game into Yale in 1894 and into the Anderson Normal School of Physical Education (now the New Haven Normal School of Physical Education). It has been impossible for me to obtain information as to just when the different colleges began to play basketball. I have written many letters in an effort to gather data on this subject, but usually I learn that the physical director during that period has long since left or is no longer living. No one seems to have kept a record of the early games.

Although the growth of basketball in the colleges was comparatively slow, it established itself on a firm basis, and by 1905 it was recognized as a permanent college winter sport. Leagues and conferences had been formed, and coaches and directors were intensely interested in the development of the game.

The general acceptance of basketball by the colleges led them to feel that they were entitled to publish their own set of rules. They felt that college basketball was on such a high plane that it was unnecessary for them to be governed by the A.A.U. In 1905, the colleges first set up their own regulations. Though I have already discussed these regulations, I should like to say here that the colleges did not, at that time, ask any other organization to accept the collegiate rules; those organizations that adopted them did so of their own free will.

The college conferences have played an important part in the control of basketball. Indeed, it would have been impossible to have the sport on a high plane had it not been for their regulations concerning eligibility and playing rules. The conferences have not been uniform, but their regulations have tended to elevate basketball to the position that it enjoys in colleges today.

There is no doubt in my mind that the finest basketball played today is in the colleges. We often hear a comparison of the merits of collegiate teams and those of the independent or professional teams. I do not claim that collegiate teams are superior to many of the independent teams, but I do believe that the college players, as a group, are far superior to any other group that may be mentioned.

In making a comparison of the college and independent teams, it will be well to ask how many of the independent players received much of their basketball training in colleges. I am sure that the percentage is very high.

While the colleges have spread the game by presenting contests before thousands of spectators, they have also developed the technique of the game to a remarkable degree. As the high schools expanded their sports, they went to the colleges to find coaches who were experts in basketball. In this manner, the college-trained players not only spread but they also developed the game. It is needless to say that most of the secondary coaches of today are far superior to the early college coaches and that there were few college teams as late as 1900 that would have a chance with the high-school basketball teams of our larger cities today.

It may seem odd that the construction of gymnasiums and field houses has affected the spread of basketball; these great buildings, however, have allowed many spectators to see the game. As a result, the enthusiasts have organized many of their own teams.

In the past few years, the colleges have also developed coaching schools. These schools, conducted by some of the outstanding coaches of the country, give the teachers from the smaller schools a chance to meet and discuss new developments of the game, such as rules and systems. Several times I have visited these schools, and I have found the discussions most interesting.

It is only fair to give due credit to the colleges for their development of basketball. I feel, however, that there is another point to be considered: colleges, at the present time, dominate the game. The number of collegiate members of the rules committee far exceeds the membership of any other organization. The colleges have taken the responsibility of regulating the game for all the institutions that are playing it. In my opinion, their control may not be beneficial to the game. It seems unfair, moreover, that the colleges should make drastic rules for themselves, then force other organizations to accept them.

With the introduction of the ten-second rule, many of the high-school and not a few of the college conferences ignored the change in play. At the present time, there is much discussion of other changes that have been suggested. Most of them are directly concerned with the colleges and take no recognition of the superior numbers who play the game in other organizations. It is my belief that if the colleges change the game, they should expressly state that many of the revisions affect only their own rules.

High Schools

If, in the coming basketball season, the papers should announce that the Holyoke, Massachusetts, High School played and defeated Dartmouth and Holy Cross Colleges, many people would be inclined to think that there must have been some mistake. In the season of 1900-1901 the Holyoke team defeated both of these teams along with some other strong teams. It was not at all uncommon for the early high-school teams to outrank the college teams.

Basketball was accepted by the high schools before the colleges took it up as an organized sport. There may be several explanations for this fact, but I believe that the younger boys who played in the Y.M.C.A. gymnasiums took the game with them into the high schools. It was only after these boys graduated from high school and entered college that basketball really began to take hold in that institution.

The first basketball league of which I have any record was in Denver, Colorado, in 1896, while I was physical director of the Y.M.C.A. As the high schools did not have a gymnasium, the games of their league were played in the "Y" gym. There were few officials at that time, and as a result I did much of this work. Many of the high-school players were also students in my Y.M.C.A. classes, and usually after a game the boys would ask me for information about their technique or play. Their enthusiasm was largely responsible for the high type of play in this league.

Though I have no definite record, I know that the game spread very rapidly in the high schools; and it was only a few years after the introduction of basketball until many high schools all over the country were playing games among themselves. Today there is no other institution that has so many teams as the high school.

A few years ago I attended an interscholastic tournament in Indianapolis, Indiana. At the most advantageous point on the floor was a row of reserved seats. On inquiring about them, I was told that these seats were reserved for the college coaches at the tournament. During the course of the evening, I noticed two of the outstanding coaches of the country carefully observing the play and taking notes. Just how much of the reputation of these men depended on their selection of future basketball players I do not know, but I think it safe to say that there are few high-school tournaments where college coaches may not be found looking for material. Under these conditions, it is clear that college basketball is largely dependent on the high schools rather than the high schools being dependent on the colleges.

When in 1898 I came to the University of Kansas, I organized a basketball team, the members of which had never seen a basketball game. Today it would be interesting to know whether there are any boys playing college basketball who did not play in high school. On checking some of the teams throughout the country, as those of the University of Minnesota, Iowa, and Kansas, I did not find any college player who had not played in high school. Most of the regular college teams are composed of men who were rated high for their ability on the high-school teams.

There is no doubt but that collegiate basketball has had a distinct effect on the present day high-school teams. Coaches who are hired from the colleges take with them the style of basketball that they have learned there. When their boys are ready to enter college, they are unusually well prepared.

Some high-school directors attend two and even three of the summer coaching schools in one season. With the knowledge of the different styles of play and the best points from each of the different styles, it is little wonder that some high-school

D'Ambra

SHE PLAYED ON THE FIRST GIRLS' TEAM—AND
MARRIED THE INVENTOR
You See Them Forty Years Later

Anderson

AT THE NATIONAL INTERCOLLEGIATE BASKETBALL
TOURNAMENT, KANSAS CITY, MARCH, 1939

coaches really know more basketball than any one of the instructors under whom they may study.

It must not be inferred that basketball is confined in the high schools to the very few teams that represent the schools. The game is used as an intramural sport as well as a class exercise. It has been estimated that 95 per cent of the high schools in this country play basketball; and if this estimate is anywhere near correct, the high schools certainly lead all other institutions in the number of players. For this reason, the various state high-school athletic associations have organized to control as well as to develop and to stabilize the game.

Mr. Arthur Trestler was largely responsible for the splendid organization of the high schools in Indiana, one of the first states to conduct a series of tournaments. The winners of these tournaments still meet in Indianapolis to play for the state title. I was invited to attend one of these tournaments, and the sight of the Indianapolis Coliseum, packed with fifteen thousand people, gave me a thrill that I shall not soon forget.

I was to speak at the final game of the tournament, and arrived at the Coliseum to find that the doors had been closed. There were no seats left, and many people were being turned away. At the door I presented a reserved seat ticket and an official's badge, only to be informed by the guard that he could allow no one to enter. I explained to him that I was to speak there that evening, but he only smiled and shook his head. As I stood there chuckling to myself, a captain of police stepped up to me and asked what the trouble was. I explained my predicament. He asked my name, and when I told him he exploded, "Good Lord, man, why didn't you say so long ago?"

Most of the states all over the country have adopted the same system that is used in Indiana, and the old system of having all the high-school teams in the state meet at one place for a grand big elimination tournament has largely been done away with. While this old system had some advantages, there were also many drawbacks. One of the older schedules lists 1,478 players as contestants in one tournament. This number was not unusually large, but it may well show the problems that arose.

Basketball has played an important part in intramural programs, and statistics (see p. 191) show that there are more teams entered in basketball than in any other sport. Not long ago I was talking to Mr. Harley Selvedge, head of the physical education department at Paseo High School, in Kansas City, Missouri. Mr. Selvedge told me that in his school there were 112 teams of six men each who played basketball in their regular classes. Beside these teams there were forty that were playing an intramural schedule in addition to the regular school team.

While I do not feel that basketball should be substituted for a physical-education course in high school, I do feel that the game supplies an interesting and profitable activity for the growing boy.

Churches

A few years ago, on a visit to my only sister I asked her if she had ever forgiven me for leaving the ministry. She looked seriously at me, shook her head and said, "No, Jim, you put your hand to the plow and then turned back." As long as she lived she never witnessed a basketball game, and I believe that she was a little ashamed to think that I had been the originator of the game.

My sister was very religious, and the attitude that she took toward sports of all kinds was not at all uncommon. I can distinctly remember in my boyhood days the concern that was felt for the men and boys who were taking part in athletics. It has only been in comparatively recent years that the churches have accepted athletics as an aid; it will never cease to be a wonder to me when I hear some athletic event announced from the pulpit.

Just how much basketball has had to do with the acceptance of athletics in the churches is a moot question. It is very likely that many of the churches realized the necessity for some activity that would keep the young people interested, and as basketball was easily learned and required little capital to outfit a team, it presented a desirable recreation. Today, there are few cities in the United States that do not sponsor a church basketball league; and in some of the larger cities, hundreds of teams are sponsored by the churches.

Probably the first church to form a basketball team was the one directed by Doctor Hall in New York City. Many times I have heard this man speak from the pulpit, and it is not a surprise to me that he was among the pioneers to foster sports for the younger people in the church. I am not sure of the exact date that this team was formed, but it was in the early part of 1897.

It was not until 1904 that a group of churches, realizing that basketball might be a distinct help, met and organized a league in New York City. Four churches were represented in this first league; since its organization, this league has probably grown to be the largest in the world. The following year, the Cleveland churches formed a league; and today there are several hundred teams in that city playing regular schedules throughout the basketball season. Today, one church league in Brooklyn, New York, consists of sixty-six teams. In Toronto, Canada, a city where only a few years ago the city fathers refused to let the street cars run on Sunday, there is a church league of seventy-five boys' teams and thirty-one girls' teams.

In 1905, the theological colleges began to take up basketball, and the development of the game in these institutions had much to do with the spread in the religious organizations. When the students graduated from these institutions and went into the field, they took with them a favorable attitude toward basketball; much credit must be given to these young men for the acceptance of sports by the churches.

While the high schools undoubtedly have the largest number of highly organized teams, churches and Sunday schools all over the country have organized teams and leagues, and the number of boys and girls that are taking part in these leagues runs into hundreds of thousands. More and more, basketball will be an opportunity of solving the problem of leisure time.

In Dallas, Texas, I was invited to witness some basketball games. I expected to see two teams in action. Imagine my surprise, on entering one of the buildings, to see ten courts laid out. I was informed that each court was used every night of the week, and that many of the teams represented churches or Sunday schools. A partition cut off about half of the courts. One section was always free to any one wishing to watch the games, and the other was used by the teams that charged admission.

Whenever I witness games in a church league, I feel that my vision, almost half a century ago, of the time when the Christian people would recognize the true value of athletics, has become a reality.

There are two other religious organizations that closely resemble the Y.M.C.A. in their objectives and methods: the Knights of Columbus and the Young Men's Hebrew Association. The Catholic institutions early took up basketball in the parish houses; Father Matthew's Temperance Societies had teams before records were kept.

The first church league was composed of Catholic teams and was organized in 1904 in New York City. The number of leagues in the Catholic churches increased rapidly for the next few years.

In answer to an inquiry, Thomas R. Hill writes concerning the Knights of Columbus:

> Basketball has been played among the various councils in Philadelphia intermittently for the past twenty years. However, with the organiza-

tion of the National Council of this society in 1921, the game was adopted as a major sport and leagues have been conducted each year since that time.

In 1923, Chicago had a Knights of Columbus league consisting of eighteen teams.

Loyola University, of Chicago, has, since 1923, held the National Catholic Interscholastic Basketball Tournament, and the number of teams in this tournament is increasing each year. These teams represent Catholic leagues of cities, states, and districts scattered over the United States.

The Young Men's Hebrew Association had many players and a number of teams in the early history of basketball. Before the spread of this organization for Jewish people, many of them made use of the Y.M.C.A. privileges. In 1915, there were thirteen cities that reported having teams or leagues playing regular schedules. In New York City there were fifteen Y.M.H.A.'s, and from these teams the Metropolitan League was formed. In 1923 the organization formed a league that was known as the Big Brother Jewish League in Philadelphia, and each year these leagues have increased in number as the game has grown in popularity among these societies. One season, the Y.M.H.A.

of Kansas City was runner-up for competition in the national tournament, representing Kansas City.

Settlement Houses

It is indeed interesting to note that the settlement houses were among the very early institutions to take up basketball.

As I sat in a National Collegiate Athletic Association meeting one day in New York City, a young man next to me leaned over, introduced himself, and asked me if I would come over to Brooklyn that evening and speak to a group of boys. I assured him that I would be delighted to do so, as I had wondered about the work that these organizations were doing.

The young man told me just how to reach the place, and as I followed those directions that evening, I found that they led me to an old gray stone church. The basement of the church was lighted, and as I made my way down the worn steps, my young acquaintance met me. He took me into the building and showed me the large gymnasium filled with benches. I had expected to see a small group of younger boys, but I soon realized that I was to talk to a large audience of boys ranging in age from twelve years to twenty—boys who were used to taking care of themselves. I noticed their alert faces—ready for any kind of fun and willing to take part in any kind of an escapade. It is seldom that I have worked harder to present the story of basketball than I did to that group. This meeting was my introduction to settlement-house work, and I began to inquire when these houses had first used the game.

According to my record, Hull House in Chicago was the first to play outside games. In 1900 it scheduled several games with outside organizations, and it found that basketball was a material help in keeping some of the boys off the streets. Several settlement houses in New York City had played for some time before this, but the competition had always been within the institution. It was not until 1903 that a permanent organization was formed for the control of basketball; today the game is considered one of the major activities in the settlement houses.

Though the game has been extensively used in connection with settlement work, it has received little publicity, because the attention has been given to the development of the boys rather than to the winning of the games.

Industrial Institutions

As the whole country has become conscious of the need for recreation, many of our large industrial institutions have set aside appropriations for it. Basketball is today the most important sport sponsored by the industries. Most large cities have industrial leagues that are of immense value, not only to the players but to the industries as well. I have seen two rival industrial teams play games that caused as much interest and feeling as most of our college games. A manufacturer in Chicago once made the statement to me that the games played between the departments of his factory did more to develop loyalty to the organization than any other factor.

As the industrial teams became highly expert, they began to travel over the country, and their sponsors realized that in the teams they had a means of advertising. The Cook Paint and Varnish team of Kansas City, known all over the United States; the Hillard Chemical Company of St. Joseph, Missouri; the Tulsa Oilers, a team that played the outstanding teams of the country; and the Wichita Henrys, at one time an outstanding team of the country—all are teams that have an amateur standing and that are sponsored by industrial institutions.

There has been some objection to the industries using basketball as an advertising medium, but I can see no foundation for it. Often when a boy graduates from college, he is given a job with some firm with the understanding that he will play on the firm's team in his spare hours. This play not only allows the boy to continue his physical activity, but also allows him the advantage of being well known. In my estimation, these are distinct advantages to the boys themselves, and hundreds of them have become highly valued members of the organizations for which they went to work. In return for the interest and money the industries have spent on teams all over the country, it is only fair that they should derive some measure of the advertising as well as the increased loyalty developed by their players.

Indian Teams

The term All American, as used in sports, usually denotes a selection of players who are supposedly the best in the United States. I have in mind a team that was composed of players who really were all Americans. Basketball among the Indians has had little publicity; yet a letter that I have from Dr. H. F. Kallenberg tells of the introduction of

basketball among the Sioux Indians in the summer
of 1892. Doctor Kallenberg says:

> In the summer of 1892 I attended, with C. K.
> Ober, conferences of Sioux Indians held at Big
> Stone Lake, South Dakota. The following sum-
> mer I attended the same conference which was
> held at Pierre. At both of these conferences
> I introduced basketball, and it was played for
> the first time by the Indians. We cut small
> saplings for uprights and in place of baskets we
> used a rim made of willows and fastened to the
> uprights. The Indians took to the game like
> ducks do to water, and soon basketball became
> their chosen form of recreation.

Carlisle was the first Indian school to play basketball, but the success that it met with there showed
that the game was especially adapted to Indian
youth. It was not long after, that U. S. G. Plank
introduced the game into Haskell Institute. During each winter I made it a point to see several
games at Haskell, because I delight in the agility of
the Indian boys.

I have talked to several coaches of Indian teams
and have found that coaching a team of Indian boys
presents several problems that are not found among
white boys. One coach told me that he had several

good players who would not take part in the sport for fear of ridicule, and that some of the boys felt it inexcusable to make a mistake. They would not run this chance before a group of people. Besides, the Indian teams are usually made up of comparatively small men. This fact is a distinct handicap to them; but their ability to move quickly and their art of deception overcome the disadvantage of their height, so that wherever these teams play they are assured of a large crowd of spectators.

I have often said the most expert dribbler that I have ever seen was Louis (Little Rabbit) Weller, of Haskell Institute. I have seen him take the ball under his own basket and weave his way in and out the entire length of the floor. It always amused spectators to see Little Rabbit take the ball and, by dribbling, challenge the much larger players to take it from him.

After a game in which I had watched Weller play, I was talking with some of the officials when someone touched me lightly on the arm. I turned to see a tall, well-built Indian boy extending his hand. Immediately my mind flashed back over the years to the time when I first came to Kansas and when this man had played guard on one of the first Haskell teams. How well I remember his superb guarding! To me this player, named Archiquette, had embodied all the requirements for a perfect guard.

Military and Naval Organizations

Since that early contest in April, 1892, between the Y.M.C.A. and the 26th Separate Company, a military organization, the military forces of the United States have continued to play basketball. The armories have supplied a place for the games, and there are few branches of the service that are not represented by hundreds of teams. The development of the game by the military forces has been in some measure responsible for the spread of basketball into the foreign countries.

After the Armistice, two teams from the American Army, one from Orly Flying Field, and the other, an artillery outfit from Bordeaux, visited the British sector to play basketball. They found that the British did not play the game because it had been introduced into England as a girls' game.

When the Americans found that there were no British teams, they played an exhibition game. At the conclusion of the exhibition, a group of British officers asked if they could not have a try at it. As these men had no basketball shoes, they borrowed them from one of the teams, and, pulling off their tunics, they started to play. The ball was tossed up and, try as they might, the Englishmen were unable to get their hands on the ball. A major who had been so cocksure that a Britisher could excel at any sport made the remark, "Why, we did not know that it was that kind of a game, or we would certainly have used it as training for bayonet practice."

The military men have always been of an athletic type, and it was natural that they would take up any form of sport that was available for winter use. Within five years after the game was started, there were eighteen military organizations playing regular schedules. National guard units, as well as the regular service, had teams, and during the nights that were not taken up by drill, the different companies or branches of the service used the armories for basketball games.

The Navy did not take up basketball so quickly as the military branches, but when it once started, it organized teams in the different yards. Soon each ship with sufficient recreation space was busy developing a team to represent it.

Both the Army and the Navy have been instrumental in spreading the game to foreign countries. As the Army is usually posted in one place longer than the Navy, it naturally has had a better chance to introduce the game into foreign lands. Both the Navy and the Marines, however, have promoted the game. Mr. R. I. Forbes, who is stationed in China, recently told me that the Marines in Peiping not only play games with the Chinese teams but also aid these teams by coaching and officiating.

THE GREEKS HAVE A WORD FOR IT TOO
An Outdoor Basketball Game at the Y.M.C.A. Field in
Salonika, Greece

THE GAME CROSSES THE PACIFIC
An Early Basketball Game in Japan

CHAPTER VIII

THE FOREIGN SPREAD

B ASKETBALL was accepted in many foreign countries soon after the game was first played in the United States. It was early introduced into several European countries, although they did not play the game so extensively as some of the far eastern nations. Even today the sport is not so popular in England as it is in China and Japan. The Y.M.C.A., which had been instrumental in spreading the game in the United States, was also largely responsible for the foreign spread through its foreign branches.

There is little doubt that the war of 1914 did much to increase the popularity of basketball in foreign countries; as a direct result of seeing the Americans play the game, it has been taken up and accepted by nations that previously knew little of basketball.

I have seen the game played in foreign countries, and I have received numerous pictures of contests and courts from Australia to Alaska. In spite of the fact that I have also written many letters trying to determine just when basketball was introduced into other countries, I have been unable to gather complete and accurate data. To attempt to state chronologically when the game was first accepted by different nations might, therefore, cause confusion. In a few instances, however, the introduction of the game is clearly set, and in some the individual who first introduced the game is known. One instance in particular is that of my native country, Canada.

Canada

If Canada may be considered as a foreign country, it indeed may claim to be the first country outside of the United States to play basketball. Of the ten men on the first team, there were five Canadians. McDonald was from Nova Scotia, Archibald and Thompson were from New Brunswick, and Patton and I from Ontario. All of these men, with the exception of myself, returned to Canada and took basketball with them.

The spread of basketball in Canada was not so rapid as it was in this country. In the first place, the Dominion was not so thickly populated as this country; and in the second place, Canada was so well adapted for outdoor winter sports that it did not feel the need for a new winter game. It has been only in the past few years that basketball has taken a firm hold in the Dominion, and today the game is widely played in all of the provinces.

The Dominion is divided into basketball districts, and the winning team from each district competes in a national tournament, the winners of which are declared national champions. In the larger Canadian cities, the churches have done much to popularize the game; and the high schools have taken it up to such an extent that there is a representative on the rules committee from that country.

Several years ago I was invited to make a trip to Edmonton, Alberta, to see the Commercial Grads, one of the outstanding girls' teams, play. Mr. and Mrs. Percival Page were in charge of the team made up of graduates of the Commercial High School in Edmonton. The girls' playing was a revelation to me; they handled the ball as the boys do, and their floor work was far superior to what I believed possible for girls. In spite of the fact that these girls played either boys' or girls' rules, they were typical young ladies, not the tomboy type at all.

Some years ago the Toilers, one of the leading boys' teams, from Winnipeg, made a trip to Tulsa, Oklahoma, to play the champions of the United States, the Diamond Oilers. The Toilers were defeated in two games and were returning by plane to resume the series at Winnipeg, when the plane crashed at Neodeasha, Kansas. Two of the players were killed, and most of the others were injured. I felt then that this accident would break up the team, but Colonel Sampson, who was in charge of the team at that time, later informed me that they were carrying on and that they again expected to have a national championship team.

Although basketball is not so far advanced in Canada as it is in the United States, I feel sure that in a few years, Canadian teams will be playing on an equal basis with other teams in the world.

Alaska

Don Alford, whom I had coached on the University of Kansas team, went to Alaska in 1906 and helped to organize a team in Nome. This Alaskan team liked the game, and with practice and coaching it became so expert that a trip through some of the States was scheduled. In spite of the fact that the players had been together through only one season, their record in the United States showed that these men from the North were as expert at basketball as our own teams. I have been unable to learn the exact number of games the Nome team won or lost, but as far as I can determine, it won more than 85 per cent of its games.

Philippine Islands

As there seems to be little to indicate exactly when basketball was introduced into the Philippine Islands, it is probable that the natives gained their first information of the game through watching the American soldiers stationed there.

It was not until 1910 that a league was definitely organized. The Manila Y.M.C.A. and the Bureau of Education both did much to promote the sport, and it is through their influence that basketball has been adopted throughout most of the twenty-one provinces. The Philippine colleges and universities are using the game as a part of their physical-education and sports program, and it has been adopted as an official event by the National Collegiate Athletic Association of the Philippine Islands.

The Far Eastern Athletic Association, which is in many ways comparable to the Olympics, lists basketball as one of its events. Competing with China, Japan, and India, the Philippines have won a good percentage of the basketball championships.

In a letter, Regino Ylanan says that the interest in basketball in the Philippine Islands is growing each year, and that the proficiency with which it is being played is showing a marked advance.

The West Indies

It has always been my opinion that basketball would not be accepted in the southern countries as readily as in the northern, because many of the southern countries can use outdoor sports the year around and because indoor exercise is not necessary. Yet many of the southern countries, as well as the smaller islands, have taken up basketball; in most instances, the game is included in the school activities.

Only recently Miss Anna McCracken, an instructor in the University of Kansas, told me that her aunt, Miss Alsina Andrews, from Hector River, Jamaica, had spoken of the popularity of basketball in Jamaica. Miss Andrews explained that most of the schools were private schools aided by the British government and that basketball was played extensively by the boys of the island. These boys are largely Indians, although there are many Negroes and some few Orientals.

In many of the smaller islands of this district where basketball is popular, the game is played entirely out of doors; the courts are the earth, pounded hard by the constant tramp of bare feet.

I have been unable to learn how old these courts are or when basketball was first played in Jamaica, but it seems that the game was well established by 1926. Haiti is well acquainted with basketball, although I cannot learn when it was introduced into this island.

Cuba, on the other hand, has quite as extensive basketball program. The game is played in the schools, and both school and independent leagues are well organized.

In Puerto Rico, basketball has become a national sport. In a letter, Julio A. Francis states that a meeting was held January 12, 1930, in Mayaguez, to form a basketball association. This meeting was largely attended by officials, sports writers, and representatives of teams. The result was the formation of the Puerto Rican Basketball Association, which elected for its officers men who were interested in the promotion of the game. I feel it a distinct compliment that, along with Theodore Roosevelt, then governor of the island, I should be elected as honorary chairman of the Association.

South America

Basketball was introduced into South America in 1896 by a missionary stationed in São Paulo, Brazil, who organized a team in McKenzie College.

This team took up the game readily and was well on the way to becoming adept at the sport. One day as the coach was working with the boys, he accidentally left a paper on his desk, and in this paper was the picture of a girls' basketball team. Some of the team saw the picture and immediately refused to play any game that was meant for girls.

Although this attitude has almost disappeared, there are a few sections of South America where the boys still refuse to play basketball. Jess Hopkins, who has done much to promote the game in South America, stated in a letter that on a trip through Brazil he found some sections where basketball was still considered a girls' game. Mr. Hopkins is known as the father of basketball on the southern continent.

In the larger cities of South America, basketball is played much as it is here. In Montevideo, Uruguay, the game is played in gymnasiums; the organization in this city compares favorably with those of our larger cities here in the United States.

Western Europe

It was a raw spring day in 1918, and the streets of Paris were damp and uninviting. As I walked along the Rue St. Michel going from my hotel to my office, I passed one of those small book shops

that are so common in France. One of these shops
I had noticed several times, and as I was early that
morning, I stepped through the crowded door into
its dim interior. Books were everywhere, old books
and new ones, classics and the cheapest novels. As
I stood in front of one of the racks, I noticed a
small red book with the chapter title "Le Basketball," in *Les Sports pour Tous* by Ern. Weber. I
bought the book and took it to the office with me.
Upon examination I found that it was a French
translation of the basketball rules. I was interested
to know when the book was printed, but I could find
no date either in the rules themselves or on the
frontispiece. When I turned to the advertisements
in the book, I found the date 1897.

There is no doubt, as I have said, that the War
had a vital influence on the spread of basketball in
the European nations. In France it was common
to see basketball goals at the American canton-
ments, and the play on these courts was always witnessed by a group of French people. I remember a
group of French soldiers watching a game. After
its finish, they took the ball and attempted to throw
it into the basket. They were at first quite awkward
in their attempts, but the rapidity with which they
learned to pass and shoot was astonishing. It was
largely through the American soldiers that the

French people became acquainted with the game as it is really played by men. Although the French girls had played basketball for some time, its popularity among the men did not come until after the Armistice.

After the Armistice was signed, the Inter-Allied Games were held in Paris, and although the Americans won the basketball title, the French and Italian teams that had recently taken up the game furnished most interesting competition.

Only recently I picked up a paper and noticed that the girls' championship team of the United States had returned from a trip to France to play the champions of that country. I had seen the American champions play and was much surprised to learn that they had been defeated by the French team and that the French women held the world championship.

Although France has wholeheartedly accepted basketball, England has shown little enthusiasm for the game. In searching for a record of some English team, I find mention only of the London Y.M.C.A., and there is little in regard to history of this group.

Soon after the origin of basketball, Miss Bessie Fotheringham went to England and introduced the girls' game. The acceptance of basketball by the girls of that country stamped the game as one that was played by women, and the English men therefore refused to play it. England has not been alone in this attitude, but it seems that most of the other countries in which basketball was introduced as a girls' game have overcome this viewpoint, and both men and women are now playing.

The Far East

While I was attending the Training School, one of my classmates, a Japanese named Ishakawa, made the first sketch of a basketball game. This drawing was printed in the guide for 1893 and has been reproduced many times. Mr. Ishakawa attended the University of Wisconsin after leaving Springfield, and, I understand, he returned to his native country soon after his graduation. Whether he introduced basketball into Japan I am unable to say; I do know that as early as 1900 Hancock, in his book on physical education in Japan, mentions basketball as an important part of the program for Japanese women.

Although basketball was undoubtedly introduced into Japan soon after its origin, it was not generally accepted as a sport for boys until about 1913, when Mr. Franklin Brown, a graduate of the Chicago Y.M.C.A. College, went to that country. Mr.

Brown organized teams and leagues in several of the larger cities, and with the help of some students who had attended school in the United States, he was successful in making the game so popular that it is played extensively throughout Japan.

The Japanese have sent several teams to the United States as well as to the Oriental Olympics. Wasida College sent a team that toured our West Coast, and a Y.M.C.A. team visited Honolulu and played a series of games. In 1933, a team from Meiji University played an exhibition game against Washburn College at Topeka, Kansas. The Japanese, although under a distinct handicap in size, were fast as lightning on the floor and handled the ball and played with astonishing agility. After this game I met the members of the team and their manager. Through their interpreter they told me that basketball was one of the leading sports of their country and that each year it was spreading rapidly.

Not only did Mr. Brown develop the game in Japan, but he made several trips into Manchuria and was instrumental in introducing the game into that country.

China was one of the first foreign nations to take up basketball, and I believe that the game was played there within a few years after its origin. Robert Gailey, who played center on the Princeton team, introduced the game into China in 1898. Although basketball was rather extensively played, it was not until several years later, when Dr. Charles Siler went to China, that the scientific type of basketball was played. Doctor Siler was an old K. U. basketball player, and it was largely owing to his efforts that the game earned the popularity that it now enjoys. In 1908, Dr. Max J. Exner went to East China as National Director for the Y.M.C.A. and spread the game in the eastern section of China through the tournaments and leagues that he organized.

A few years ago I received an interesting letter from Mr. M. V. Ambros, who was traveling through China and was in Peiping at the time he wrote. Mr. Ambros says:

> We remember you very often, Dr. Naismith, while looking from the train or riding in a rickasha. In all parts of different cities we saw basketball goals everywhere. It will be a real pleasure for you to travel through the orient to see how much basketball is really played. It cannot be described or pictured; it cannot be told; it must be seen.
>
> Just recently we saw the girls' league playing at Peiping "Y" gymnasium. Lots of spectators from all kinds of social levels, coolies beside the soldiers, and the family carrying a baby in hands,

the referee in a long Chinese skirt or coat, the encouragement of the players by the crowd around. You can just feel what the game means to them.

India is another of the Far East group that has organized basketball, and from that country comes the report of the Bengal Basketball Association. This Association came into existence at a meeting called by Mr. M. J. Mukerjee, director of physical education of the Calcutta Y.M.C.A. The official playing code, as promulgated by the basketball rules committee, has been adopted by the Bengal Association. Nineteen organizations are represented in the Bengal Association, and I understand that this group meets annually.

In 1920, H. C. Buck wrote from Madras, India, that in his city a school of physical education had been opened and that physical directors were being trained for all parts of India, Burma, and Ceylon. He added that basketball had become an important sport of these countries and that it was sure to make progress in the schools and colleges as well as in the Y.M.C.A.

While mentioning basketball in the Far East it may be well to mention some of the other distant countries that have taken up the game. Down off the east coast of Africa, Madagascar received the game from the French soldiers stationed at that place. Though the people of this island were acquainted with the game, it was not until Eugene Beigbeder went there in 1924 that basketball was really organized. Today it is played in the schools and forms an important part of the sports program of that country.

In the southern part of Asia there are several countries that have not only adopted basketball but have also translated the rules into their own languages.

The Near East

In 1924, I received a letter from Chester K. Tobin, who was connected with the Y.M.C.A. in Turkey. I knew Mr. Tobin here in the United States before he went to Constantinople, and I was pleased to hear that the Turkish people were translating the basketball rules into their language. The letter from Mr. Tobin asked if I would write a message to the boys of Turkey, to be printed in the front of the rule book.

At the time I received the letter, I was in a camp in the Rocky Mountains, and I answered on the only available paper that I could find, a few sheets of foolscap. Several months later I received a copy of the basketball rules from Constantinople, and in the front of the book was my picture and the message that I had written. I had not kept a copy of my letter to Tobin, and I never knew just what I said.

Egypt is another country that has developed basketball to an astonishing degree. A recent picture that I received from Cairo shows a group of boys playing on an open court and clad only in shorts.

G. M. Tamblyn is largely responsible for the introduction of the game into Egypt, and his interest and work in this country have resulted in the games being taken up by the schools and in the formation of leagues. In 1925, Mr. Tamblyn, along with Dr. William A. Eddy, of Cairo University, formed the Egyptian Basketball Union; today this organization largely controls the sport, especially around Cairo. At the time of its conception, the Union had as an ideal the spread of basketball throughout the nation, and it is largely owing to the influence of this organization that basketball has attained the status that it has there.

Syria is another country that has used basketball as a recreation for many years. In 1901, Joseph A. Goodhue, who was physical instructor at the Protestant College in Beirut, organized eight teams in the college and arranged a tournament. A letter written in 1929 related that the game had become

THE FIRST TOSS-UP—CHINA vs. JAPAN
Far Eastern Championship Games, Osaka, Japan, May, 1923

THE STORY GOES AROUND THE WORLD

so popular that many institutions were building athletic fields and installing basketball courts.

Central and Southern Europe

In recent years Czechoslovakia had advanced rapidly in the number of teams that were playing basketball. F. M. Marek was instrumental in pushing the game in that country, and his interest and work was a decided help in the formation of a basketball league in the European countries.

While the game was played by both boys and girls, the lack of adequate facilities kept the game from spreading rapidly. Prague was probably the basketball center of the nation, and basketball was a part of the activity program of the schools in this city.

That basketball is taking a firm hold in the southern European countries is clearly indicated by a meeting that was called in Geneva, Switzerland, in 1932. In this year, representatives from ten countries met at the First International Basketball Conference. The Conference was called as a result of a request by the National Basketball Federation of Czechoslovakia, Portugal, and Switzerland.

The meeting was called as a result of the general dissatisfaction that existed because of the variations of the rules and the lack of a uniform playing code; the outcome of the Conference was the formation of the International Federation of Basketball. The ten countries represented in this Federation were Czechoslovakia, Portugal, Switzerland, Latvia, Italy, Argentina, Greece, Hungary, Bulgaria, and Rumania. They adopted the rules that are used here in the United States with a few variations to meet the national conditions of the countries mentioned.

One interesting fact about the conference was that, although France was invited to attend, that country was not represented. A statement was made that France was unwilling to change the rules that were used in that country, and a separate conference was held in Paris. This conference was rather a national meeting, and none of the nations represented in the International Federation of Basketball were present at the Paris meeting.

There is every indication that some of the countries that do not play basketball at the present time will soon take it up. In 1936, basketball was included for the first time in the Olympic Games, in Berlin. There is little doubt that this did much to increase the interest in basketball over the entire world.

CHAPTER IX

THE DEVELOPMENT OF GIRLS' BASKETBALL

ALTHOUGH basketball was originated in a men's institution, it was scarcely a month old when it was taken up by girls. Badminton, cycling, and sometimes tennis were considered correct sports for girls at that time. The gymnasium in which basketball was originated, as I have said before, was in a basement, and a door led from the balcony directly to the sidewalk. One day some young women teachers from the Buckingham Grade School passed the gymnasium on their way to lunch. Hearing the shouts in the gymnasium, they stepped through the door into the balcony to see just what was causing the commotion. They discovered a basketball game in progress; it was only a few minutes until they were clapping and cheering for one side or the other.

The visit to the gymnasium became a daily occurrence for the teachers, and about two weeks after they had first come, a group of them asked me why girls could not play basketball. I told them that I would find an hour in which the gym was not in use, if they would like to try the game. The girls were enthusiastic, and the hour was set.

When the time arrived, the girls appeared at the gymnasium, some with tennis shoes, but the majority with street shoes. None of them changed from their street clothes, costumes which were not made for freedom of movement. I shall never forget the sight that they presented in their long trailing dresses with leg-of-mutton sleeves, and in several cases with the hint of a bustle. In spite of these handicaps, the girls took the ball and began to shoot at the basket. None of the other fundamentals was observed; often some girl got the ball and ran half way across the floor to shoot at the basket.

The practice of this group was very regular, and it was not long before some of the girls became proficient at the game. The team practiced passing and shooting until it decided that it would like some competition. Other teachers were brought in, and two girls' teams were formed.

In March, 1892, the boys were conducting a basketball tournament, and among the spectators were many women. At the conclusion of the boys' play, it was suggested that the girls have a tournament. A team was organized from a group of stenographers; but since there were not enough of them, some of the wives of the faculty were asked to play. One young lady who took a prominent part on the newly organized team was a Miss Sherman, whom I later asked to become Mrs. Naismith. Throughout her life she remained actively interested in the game, and often commented on the progress the game had made.

The contest between the two girls' teams was the first really scheduled game. Soon afterward the game for girls began to spread almost as rapidly as the boys' game.

In 1893, a physical-education convention was held in the Yale gymnasium, and among the directors at this convention was Miss Senda Berensen, the director of physical education at Smith College. She became greatly interested in the game, and I told her that the girls in Springfield were playing it. Miss Berensen spent some time studying basketball in order that she might introduce it at Smith.

The Springfield *Republican*, in 1893, printed an article about a game that had been played between the freshman and sophomore teams at Smith College. No men spectators were allowed at this game, as the girls wore bloomers. Evidently much preparation had been made for the game, for the article describes the manner in which the gymnasium was decorated. One side was draped with green bunting, and the other side was trimmed with lavender flags. Large bows of the class colors were tied on each goal. The class of '96 encouraged their team with words to the tune of "Long, Long Ago," while the class of '95 answered with the song, "Hold the Fort."

Bryn Mawr took up basketball; and in a letter to A. A. Stagg, his sister, who was attending that school, described the popularity of the game.

In my scrapbook is a letter from Mrs. H. L. Carver, of Greenville, Texas, dated April 20, 1893. Mrs. Carver asked for the details of the game in order to introduce it into that state. There is little doubt that Mrs. Carver introduced basketball into Texas. A few years ago, in Dallas, I was much impressed with the type of basketball that the girls were playing. I have often used data obtained on that visit in citing the good that basketball has done for girls.

Miss Strickland, who was a graduate of the Sargent Normal School, introduced the game in Denver, Colorado. In 1896, I was invited to attend a girls' game at Wolfe Hall. The reporter who covered the game was somewhat of an artist, and a sketch that was printed in the paper the following day clearly shows a very good likeness of Bishop Spalding and me as spectators.

A quotation from the Denver *News* of February 1, 1896, describes the game in this manner:

> The two captains were Miss Adeline Rockwell, commander of the blues, and Miss Anna Ryan, captain of the reds, and the battle raged fiercely. The ball flew about in a most astounding way, lighting on the heads of the just and the unjust, for once it came down with a resounding whack upon the venerable head of Bishop Spalding and once it grazed the *News* reporter. It is a light ball, and no harm was done.

While basketball was being adopted by many of the girls' colleges, Miss Clara Baer, of Newcomb College, was experimenting with the game in an effort to eliminate some of the most strenuous parts. Miss Baer modified the game so much that the only things left were the ball and the goals. From her work were developed the nine court game, captain ball, and several other variations.

In 1895, Miss Baer published a set of rules that contained several modifications of the boys' rules. One of these modifications was the division of the court into three sections. This division came about in an interesting way. On one of the diagrams of the court there appeared a dotted line running

across the court in two places.　This line was meant
to describe the positions of the players, but it was
taken as a restraining line and was introduced,
therefore, into the girls' game.

By 1898, the game had become so popular as a
sport for girls that a group met in New York City
to discuss a set of rules for them.　This group felt
that the game, as it was played by the boys, was
too strenuous for girls; for this reason it accepted
the following modifications of the boys' rules:

1. The ball could not be taken away from the
player who was holding it.

2. The player in possession of the ball could
not hold it longer than three seconds.

3. The floor was divided into three sections,
and a player could not cross these lines under
penalty of a foul.

4. A defending player could not reach over
another player who was in possession of the ball.
The arms must be kept in a vertico-lateral plane,
and a violation of this rule by a defensive player
was called overguarding.

The natural tendency was for the girls to follow
the ball, and the constant running up and down the
floor exhausted the players quickly.　Another factor was that girls were not developed reflexly in
sports as the boys were, and it was difficult for them
to make their judgments and to act quickly.　To

meet this condition, the three-second interval was introduced. The overguarding clause was put in because of the three-second interval. If a girl were allowed three seconds in which to play the ball, it was necessary that she have at least an opportunity to pass in these three seconds.

In recent years there has been some attempt by certain girls' teams to return to the boys' style of play. It is true that many of the restrictions that were necessary in the early stages of the game are not necessary today, but I firmly believe that the girls' game, as it is played today, is a much better game for the girls than the boys' game is for the girls.

On witnessing the National Girls' Tournament that was held at Wichita, Kansas, recently, I was forced to admit that I had not seen a boys' game during the entire season that would compare in speed, accuracy of passing, and team work with that of the girls. The boys' game is not adapted for girls' play, and there was little interest shown at the tournament in the teams that played the boys' rules.

There has been some controversy in regard to the suits that are worn by many of the girls' basketball teams. To play the game, freedom of movement is necessary, and the suits now worn are far more conducive to activity than the high shoes and bustles of yesterday.

The first set of girls' rules was printed in 1898. Several times since then the rules have been revised. The girls' rules are now printed yearly.

Basketball was played very early on the Pacific Coast, and a description of a game between the University of California and Leland Stanford appears in the San Francisco *Examiner* for April 5, 1895. Even the headlines of this article were, to say the least, amusing.

WATERLOO FOR BEREKLEY GIRLS
Stanford's Fair Basketball Players
Won by a Goal.

'TWAS A HOMERIC CONTEST AND
THE BEST TEAM TRIUMPHED.

*Clad in Bloomers and Sweaters Muscular
Maidens Struggle for Supremacy*

Such headlines appeared in many papers all over the country as basketball was enthusiastically received by the girls. It was really the first chance that they had to participate in an active sport. The gentle art of cycling, along with badminton, was doomed to be displaced by activities such as basketball.

Not only in this country was basketball accepted by the women, but in many foreign countries it was also introduced as a woman's game. I have already said that the introduction into England as a girls' game has had much to do with the present attitude of the English men toward the game.

In my estimation, girls have made far greater strides in physical education in the past twenty-five years than boys. The development of sportsmanship in women is to be marveled at. I can well remember officiating at a girls' game in Springfield. When a foul was called, it was a signal for a violent argument with the player. During the entire tournament at Wichita, however, I did not see any girl openly object to a decision of a referee.

Not only have the girls developed in sportsmanship, but they have developed also in reflexes, muscular control, and judgment. A clipping in my scrapbook describes Miss Dorothy Compston, of Warwick, Rhode Island, as shooting forty-nine goals in one game. This number of goals would have been considered almost impossible in the early stages of the game. Many of the games of the early time ended with scores as low as three to one or even one to nothing.

I have often been asked what I think of men coaching girls' teams. This question is one that has been much debated, and I feel that the girls' use of boys' rules was due to the fact that the coaches were men. Regardless of who coaches the technique of the game, there should be some competent woman directly in charge of the girls. No game should be placed before the welfare of the girls.

CHAPTER X

THE PHYSIOLOGY OF BASKETBALL

THERE is a popular impression, especially among spectators, that basketball is a most strenuous game. This impression at one time was so strong that many people felt that basketball was too severe a game to be played by young people, and especially by girls. The idea that the game is too strenuous has come largely from people who watch the game. It is only natural that these people follow the ball constantly and see action wherever the ball is, judging, therefore, that all the players are constantly in action. Many have taken the attitude not only that basketball is a strenuous game, but also that it may be injurious to those who play. I shall show later that the game is not injurious.

Doctor McCurdy, of Springfield College, was of the opinion that basketball was too strenuous, and he decided to conduct experiments to determine its effect on the players. Examinations were given to the men after a game, and the results seemed to verify his belief. Albumin and casts were found in an astonishing number of cases. Doctor McCurdy published the findings of the experiment in his book on the physiology of exercise, and some people accepted these findings as proof of their contention that the game was too strenuous.

I read his report, and I determined that if they were correct and if no other factor had entered, basketball indeed should be more closely studied. If a majority of players showed albumin, blood, and casts after playing in one game, what then would be the effect on the young men that were taking part in tournaments all over the country? I determined to carry out a series of experiments under the most severe conditions that I could find.

The opportunity to do this work presented itself when the State High School Tournament was played at the University of Kansas. Many teams would take part in this tournament, and the boys, playing game after game under unnatural conditions, would show the effects if the game were too strenuous. Mr. C. E. Rowe, who was a student in the department of physical education at that time, assisted me in the experiment.

The object of the experiment was to examine the two teams that would play in the final game. We wanted a urinalysis of the men on these teams, for we felt that after having gone through the entire tournament and after having played in the final game, they would surely indicate any harmful effects. In order to get a test of these two teams, it was necessary to obtain a specimen from the players of every team that won. To Mr. Rowe fell the task, and throughout the four days of play, his work was invaluable.

After hundreds of tests had been run, we began to realize that our results were going to be different from those of Doctor McCurdy. Team after team that we examined showed little or no abnormal condition, and it soon appeared that we were to upset some of the fixed ideas about the strenuousness of basketball.

When it became evident that our results were radically different, I was afraid that there might be a feeling that the results were not exactly fair because of my relationship to the game. With this thought in mind, I turned over the specimens to the department of physiological chemistry in the University. The findings of these experts so closely coincided with my own that I was assured that our work was authentic and that the findings might be published. The results of the experiment appeared in the guide for 1925, and they had much to do with dispelling the belief that basketball was an exceptionally strenuous game.

In spite of the tests that I had made, some persons still felt that tournament play might be harmful. Indiana, one of the leading states in basketball, decided to carry on experiments similar to mine at its state tournament. A group of doctors was selected to make the tests under the most critical conditions. The findings of this group definitely settled the fact that basketball in itself is not in any way a harmful game.

The tests we made were the same that were used in life insurance examinations. Both the cold nitric and the heat tests were used for albumin, and if either of these showed the slightest trace, the case was considered positive. Benedict's solution was used for the sugar tests, and the slightest signs were given preference.

Some time before, LaGrange had made an experiment in which he found an excessive amount of urea in untrained persons after they had indulged in severe exercise. To check this result, we also included a test for urea. The Doremus ureometer was used, and after several hundreds of tests had been made without confirming LaGrange's findings, we decided to discontinue this phase of the experiment.

The examination for blood casts was made after the final game only. We decided that the maximum of strain would be shown in the final game, after

URINALYSIS OF MEMBERS OF HIGH-SCHOOL TEAMS IN
TOURNAMENT, MARCH 27, 1925

	NEWTON TEAM			
	Albumin	*Sugar*	*Blood*	*Casts*
Forney..................	Neg.	Neg.	Neg.	Neg.
Clawson.................	Neg.	Neg.	Neg.	Neg.
Gray	1 plus	Neg.	Neg.	Neg.
Trout...................	Neg.	Neg.	Neg.	5 counted
Hoover.................	Neg.	Neg.	Neg.	Neg.
Morgan.................	Neg.	Neg.	Neg.	Neg.
Okerberg...............	Neg.	Neg.	Neg.	Neg.
Cox....................	Neg.	Pos.	Neg.	Neg.
	WICHITA TEAM			
Churchill................	Neg.	Neg.	Neg.	5 counted
Bennington.............	Neg.	Neg.	Neg.	Neg.
Crossett................	Neg.	Pos.	Neg.	Neg.
McCormac..............	Neg.	Neg.	Neg.	Neg.
Fullington..............	Neg.	Pos.	Neg.	Neg.
Fowler.................	Neg.	Neg.	Neg.	Neg.
McBurney..............	Neg.	Neg.	Neg.	2 counted
Dunham................	Neg.	Neg.	Neg.	Neg.

Urine collected after each game.
Urinalysis made by E. R. Lehnken, Department of Biochemistry.
Test for albumin: Cold Nitric and Heat.
Test for sugar: Benedict's Solution.

both teams had gone through the entire tournament. The results of the experiment are shown in the accompanying chart, and a record of the actual tests that were made in the urinalysis may be found in the appendix.

As the results of our experiment had differed radically from those of the earlier experiments, I sought explanation for these differences. After much study, I came to the following conclusions:

1. That youth is not so seriously affected by physical activity as the adult.
2. That the mature students were so drilled that they could push themselves in both their practice and their games more than the younger players.
3. That the amount of food eaten and the amount of outside work done might aid in the production of albumin.
4. That high-school players were cared for, they were put to bed and rested between games, their diet was carefully selected, and their sleep was carefully prescribed.
5. That Hill's investigation on muscle recovery offered another solution.

Hill's investigation showed that the waste products of muscular activity are restored, to be again used in energy-producing materials. Lactic acid, which is produced in muscle activity, will, during the resting period, be resynthesized into glycogen in the muscle, itself, without being thrown out and new glycogen being introduced into the body. Under these conditions, the rest between the games allows the body to recover entirely.

Gould makes the statement that complete recovery from strenuous activity may be consummated in one and a half hours of rest.

It is possible that any one, or a combination, of all of the foregoing factors may explain the differences in the results of the various experiments.

I have said that many people thought that the players were in constant motion during a basketball game. In reality, there are few games, indeed, in which players are in constant action.

In gathering the statistics for the foregoing statements, we observed a series of games of the Interscholastic League of Kansas City, Missouri, through the seasons of 1925, 1926, and 1927, and at the University of Kansas during 1931 and 1932. We used stop watches to keep track of the time when the teams were in action, relaxation, and rest. We took not only the activity time of the teams but also the average activity time for different positions. Sometimes the player time ran as low as 30 per cent, as in the position of the guards.

A chart of the division of time in a championship game at the University of Kansas clearly shows the amount of rest and relaxation in comparison with the amount of activity.

The statistics for the activity of different players were taken at games played in the Interscholastic

League of Kansas City, Missouri. The accompanying chart shows the division of time for high-school players in their different positions.

TEAM ACTIVITY CHART

Elapsed time of game.........................	1 hour, nine minutes
Total activity time...........................	34 minutes, 56 seconds
Number of activity periods....................	44
Longest time of activity.......................	2 minutes, 23 seconds
Shortest time of activity......................	4 seconds
Average time of activity......................	47.6 seconds
Total relaxation time.........................	4 minutes, 38 seconds
Number of relaxation periods..................	26
Longest time of relaxation....................	17 seconds
Shortest time of relaxation...................	6 seconds
Average time of relaxation....................	10 seconds
Total time out...............................	29 minutes
Number of time outs..........................	16
Longest time out (between halves).............	10 minutes
Shortest time out............................	10 seconds
Average time out *...........................	1 minute, 11 seconds

Activity time: Time while the ball was in play.
Relaxation time: Time while the timer's watch was not stopped, but while the ball was dead.
Time out: Time while the ball was dead and the timer's watch was stopped.

This chart was made from statistics obtained at a championship game between the University of Kansas and the University of Nebraska in 1925. Although the figures fail to check by a few seconds, the difference is so slight that it may easily be ignored. It was found impossible to make the figures absolutely accurate, as the fraction of a second was disregarded.

* The average time out does not include the interval between halves.

When we realize that there are many factors that may affect the playing time of the participants, it is easy to see that basketball is not so strenuous as some people have imagined it to be. A player may be on the floor through a whole game, but such an instance is the exception rather than the rule. It is common to see as many as eight or ten substitutions

POSITION CHART

INTERSCHOLASTIC GAME, KANSAS CITY, MISSOURI, 1926

	Playing Time	Actual Time	Activity Time
Center.................	10′	15′	5′ 39″
Center.................	10′	12′ 5″	5′ 10″
Forward...............	10′	12′	7′ 21″
Forward...............	10′	15′	4′ 27″
Forward...............	10′	13′	5′ 30″
Guard.................	10′	14′	4′ 55″
Guard.................	10′	14′	3′ 40″
Average..............	10′	13′ 35″	5′ 03″

The game was played in ten-minute quarters. The watch was put on the individual player, and when he was active, the watch was running; when he was inactive, the watch was stopped.

during a game, and frequently I have seen whole new teams take the floor. All of these circumstances tend to cut down even further the activity time of the individual player. With the true conditions shown, I can see no reason for anyone's objecting to the game of basketball as too strenuous.

Basketball, in my opinion, is one of the few team games that emphasizes agility, speed, and accuracy, and is directly opposed to bodily contact. There is no necessity for the bodily shock that is part of football, hockey, and some of the other games.

It is true that, in certain parts of the country, this contact game is somewhat in vogue, and there is little doubt that this type of game is more strenuous than the open free game that is played in many sections. The style of game largely depends upon the coaches and the officials who work the game. If the rules are interpreted as they are meant to be, I believe that I could recommend basketball for any normal boy or girl.

CHAPTER XI

THE VALUES OF BASKETBALL

JOHNNY WILLIAMS had lost his temper again. I watched him come off the floor scowling and belligerent and take his seat on the side lines. It wasn't the first time that Johnny had been banished from the game; in fact, there were few games in which he was able to play the entire time without getting into trouble.

In 1896, in Denver, Colorado, I was coaching a group of teams in the Y.M.C.A., and among those was one made up entirely of printers. Johnny Williams, a short, stocky, red-haired Welshman, was a guard on the printers' team. He was an excellent player, and time after time he would play brilliant ball; but eventually he would lose his temper and be told to leave the floor, many times when he was most needed.

As I watched Johnny leave the floor in this particular game, I decided that I should talk with him. After the game, I asked him to come into the office. When he entered, he was still resentful toward the circumstances that had caused him to leave the game. He scowled at me, ready to take the reprimand that he expected, but still unwilling to admit that he was wrong.

I told him that he was a good player and that there were few guards that were his equal, but that he was really a detriment to his team. He looked at me, and his eyes snapped. Disregarding his expression, I told him that, if he was ever to be a success in basketball or in life, he must learn to control his feelings. Before he left the office, he agreed to try to control himself.

A short time later, he found, when a foul was called on him, that self-control paid. He started toward the official to protest; then suddenly he remembered his resolution and trotted away, with his face as red as his hair. The next few plays saw Johnny all over the court; he was offense and defense both, and I knew that through this physical effort he was working off his resentment.

By the end of the season he had so successfully learned to control his feelings that he was the mainstay of the team; his mates unanimously elected him captain for the following year.

Years later, on a visit to Denver, I spent some time with Johnny, who was then attending a session of the legislature as a representative from that district. He asked me if I remembered what I had told him in the office that day, and said that it had helped him to overcome a fault that would have been a serious drawback throughout his life.

I realize, through such an experience, the great amount of good that we can do through our athletics and physical education. It is only natural that I should spend much time in determining just what part basketball is playing in this program. The decisions that I have reached in regard to the game are that it is not now and it was never intended to be a complete system of physical education.

The main purpose of the game is recreation and the development of certain attributes that are peculiar to the game. Basketball was intended primarily for young men who had acquired their physical development but who were in need of exercise that would stress the skills and agile movements that were lacking in manual labor.

Because it is interesting, the game has often been substituted for all other forms of motor activity. This substitution is a grave error with young boys who have not already acquired their muscular development.

Basketball, however, has a definite place in a program of physical education: first, because it is attractive; and second, because it develops certain attributes. The game mainly develops control of nerves rather than a rugged physique.

Games have been called the laboratory for the development of moral attributes; but they will not, of themselves, accomplish this purpose. They must be properly conducted by competent individuals. Under such leadership, I believe the following attributes can be developed by basketball.

1. *Initiative,* the ability to meet new conditions with efficiency. In basketball, it is impossible to tell what an expert opponent will do; consequently, a player must react to the conditions without time for deliberation. When he meets an entirely new condition, he can not depend on the coach, but must face the emergency himself. I consider initiative one of the most valuable atributes, and the present tendency of the player to depend on the coach for his next move largely destroys the opportunity of acquiring this quality.

2. *Agility,* the power of the body to put itself into any position with quickness and ease. It is especially developed by the movements of the body in eluding an opponent, in keeping the ball away from him, and in getting into a position to make a pass, to shoot, or to dribble.

3. *Accuracy,* the ability to do the exact thing that is attempted. Basketball goals are made by passing

a ten-inch ball through an eighteen-inch opening. In order to do so, it is necessary to give the ball the right direction, elevation, and impetus. It is the accuracy with which the acts are done that determines basketball games.

4. *Alertness,* the ready response to a stimulus. In some games there may be a letting down of attention, as no further activity may occur until a signal is given. In basketball, the attention must respond instantly and at any time. The ball travels so fast and changes hands so rapidly that every player must be ready to act while the ball is in play.

5. *Co-operation,* working with teammates without definite plans from the coach. In no other game is co-operation so necessary. There are only five players on a basketball team, and each of these is dependent on the others. Five men co-operating can always beat four, and if during a game one player fails to work with his mates, he places them at a serious disadvantage.

6. *Skill,* the ability to use the correct muscle group at the right time, in the proper sequence, and with the correct amount of force, while handling a movable object with moving teammates and against moving opponents. Basketball presents these con-

ditions better than any other game, with the possible exception of hockey or lacrosse.

7. *Reflex judgment,* the ability to have the body perform the correct movement without mental process. In basketball, the eye sees an open space toward which a teammate is running, and the ball is automatically passed to him without deliberation. No prettier sight can be seen in athletics than a basketball player tipping the ball to a teammate, he, in turn, tipping it to a third mate who, while high in the air, tosses it into the goal. The whole action may take place more quickly than the mind could possibly devise the play.

8. *Speed,* the ability to move from one location to another in the shortest possible time. Basketball is a series of sprints rather than continuous running. According to our experiments, an average player is in action less than 40 per cent of the actual playing time. When he does move, however, it must be at a maximum speed. This speed entails quick starting and rapid movement, as a man may need to change his course to avoid another player coming at any angle into his path.

9. *Self-confidence,* the consciousness of ability to do things. Each player must be able to "carry on" by himself when the occasion requires. There are times when he cannot depend on his teammates to do

things, even though they are better qualified than he is. When these times arrive, he must feel able to cope with the situation.

10. *Self-sacrifice,* a willingness to place the good of the team above one's personal ambitions. The unit in basketball is the team rather than the individual player. The player who attempts to get personal glory at the sacrifice of the game is a hindrance to any team. There is no place in basketball for the egotist.

11. *Self-control,* the subordination of one's feelings for a purpose. The player who permits his feelings to interfere with his reflexes is not only a hindrance to his team, but he is also occupying a place that might better be filled by another. There are so few players on a team that one player not doing his best is a greater reduction in the relative strength of the team than in a game where there are more players involved.

12. *Sportsmanship,* the player's insistence on his own rights and his observance of the rights of others. It is playing the game vigorously, observing the rules definitely, accepting defeat gracefully, and winning courteously. Basketball is peculiarly adapted to the development of this trait because the players, officials, coaches, and spectators are in

such close proximity that an action of one is observed by the others.

Both of the contesting teams occupy the same space on the floor, and often the teams are so intermingled that it is hard to distinguish one from the other. To obey the rules that have been set down, and to recognize the rights of the opposing players under these conditions, demands the highest type of sportsmanship.

The official is often no closer to some of the plays than the spectators, and it is evident that he must practice the strictest impartiality. He must be competent to judge reflexly and have the courage to disregard any personal feelings that he might have.

The coach is not only the inspiration of the team, but he also indirectly affects the attitude of the crowd. On him falls much of the burden of establishing a sportsmanlike attitude in both the players and the spectators. Any breach of ethics on his part is immediately noted by all who may be attending the game.

Last of all, the spectators are so close to the field of play that it is often necessary for them to curb their feelings. There is no player who never makes a slip, there is no official who is always right, and there is no coach who, in the heat of a hard-fought game, may not momentarily lose his stoical attitude and commit himself in regard to some decision that he may feel is unjust.

"Booing" by the spectators of basketball has caused some comment in the past few years. I, too, have condemned the practice; but one comes to realize that we have been so proficient in teaching the game that many of the spectators are very well versed in the technique, and that it is against human nature to expect these people to sit passively and accept some decision that they honestly feel to be unjust. I believe, however, that the less attention paid to the practice of "booing," the sooner it will cease.

I may say in conclusion: Let us all be able to lose gracefully and to win courteously; to accept criticism as well as praise; and last of all, to appreciate the attitude of the other fellow at all times.

APPENDIX

A. STATISTICS ON INTRAMURAL ATHLETICS

In a recent bulletin published and edited by Fred Turbyville under the heading of *Intramural Athletics*, a supplement to *The Blue Book of College Athletics for 1932–1933*, the following figures are given in regard to the number of students that take part in different intramural sports. The data were supplied by two hundred fifty-five colleges, and clearly show that basketball is far in the lead in popularity as an intramural sport.

Basketball	32,467	Speedball	2,925
Track	22,665	Indoor ball	2,718
Baseball	21,889	Hockey	2,236
Tennis	17,549	Touch football	1,700
Swimming	13,357	Rifle	1,509
Football	12,517	Touchball	1,364
Volleyball	12,268	Indoor relay	1,253
Handball	10,862	Softball	994
Wrestling	10,752	Diamond ball	979
Golf	10,316	Ping pong	936
Boxing	9,932	Kittenball	876
Playground ball	8,306	Cake race	600
Cross country	7,881	Crew	524
Soccer	7,472	Mushball	419
Squash	6,429	Archery	326
Fencing	6,355	Pistol	281
Water polo	5,898	Winter sports	253
Gymnastics	5,580	Horseback riding	230
Horseshoes	5,507	Quoits	204
Bowling	3,298	Badminton	171
Free throw	3,148	Lacrosse	170

Not only in the number of players participating does basketball lead, but also in the number of institutions that include this sport on their intramural program. There are 241 schools in which basketball is played in intramurals, whereas the next sport, track, is included in 206 schools.

B. URINALYSIS OF BASKETBALL TEAMS TAKEN AFTER EACH
GAME IN THE STATE TOURNAMENT AT THE UNIVERSITY OF
KANSAS, MARCH 27, 1925

Name	*Albumen*	*Sugar*	*Specific Gravity*	*Color*	*Acid*	*Blood*	*Casts*	*Urea*
GRAY.....	trace	neg.	1016	amber	pos.	neg.		.0027
	trace	neg.	1025	"	"			.0024
	neg.	neg.	1022	"	"			.0021
	neg.	neg.						
(P. Chem)	neg.	neg.				neg.	neg.	
	1. Plus							
CLAWSON..	neg.	neg.	1020					.0024
	neg.	neg.	1018					.0018
	neg.	neg.	1014					.0014
	neg.	neg.						
(P. Chem)	neg.	neg.				neg.	neg.	
HOOVER...	neg.	trace	1024					.0025
	neg.	neg.	1027					
	neg.	neg.	1024					.0023
	neg.	neg.						
(P. Chem)	neg.	neg.				neg.	neg.	
COX......	neg.	neg.	1016					.0027
	trace	trace	1020					.0029
	trace	neg.	1018					.0023
	neg.	neg						
(P. Chem)	neg.	pos.				neg.	neg.	
TROUT....	neg.	neg.	1012					.0015
	neg.	neg.	1016					.0020
	neg.	neg.	1016					
	neg.	neg.						
(P. Chem)	neg.	neg.				neg.	5 counted	
FORNEY...	neg.	neg.	1012	amber	pos.			.0017
	neg.	neg.	1021	"	"			.0018
	neg.	neg.	1020	"	"			.0020
	neg.	neg.						
(P. Chem)	neg.	neg.				neg.	neg.	

B. URINALYSIS OF BASKETBALL TEAMS TAKEN AFTER EACH
GAME IN THE STATE TOURNAMENT AT THE UNIVERSITY OF
KANSAS, MARCH 27, 1925—*Continued*

Name	Albumen	Sugar	Specific Gravity	Color	Acid	Blood	Casts	Urea
OKERBERG.	neg.	neg.	1020	dark	pos.			.0025
	neg.	trace	1030	dark	"			.0031
	neg.	neg.	1011	amber	"			.0014
	neg.	neg.						
(P. Chem)	neg.	neg.				neg.	neg.	
MORGAN...	neg.	pos.	1018	straw	pos.			.0017
	neg.	neg.	1016	"	"			.0013
	neg.	neg.	1020	"	"			.0022
	neg.	neg.						
(P. Chem)	neg.	neg.				neg.	neg.	

C. SUBSTITUTION CHART

A factor that minimizes the strain is the opportunity for substitution of players. The substitutions in one game during the season of 1925–1926 are shown as follows:

Time	Substitute	Team Playing	Position	College	Length of time in the game
7:33		Ackerman	Forward	K.U.	55
		Engle	Forward	K.U.	17
		Peterson	Center	K.U.	40
		Gordon	Guard	K.U.	21
		Belgard	Guard	K.U.	54
				(visiting team)	
		Fisher	Forward	Ames	40
		Anderson	Forward	Ames	40
		Jacobson	Center	Ames	55
		Miller	Guard	Ames	49
		Arnold	Guard	Ames	55
7:42	Schmidt for	Engle	Forward	K.U.	12
7:52	Wilkins for	Gordon	Guard	K.U.	34
8:00 8:10	The half				
8:23	Engle for	Schmidt	Forward	K.U.	
8:23	Campbell for	Peterson	Center	K.U.	7
8:23	Wright for	Fisher	Forward	Ames	15
8:23	Coe for	Anderson	Forward	Ames	15
8:30	Peterson for	Campbell	Center	K.U.	
8:30	Schmidt for	Engle	Forward	K.U.	
8:32	Fisher for	Miller	Guard	Ames	
8:36	Zuber for	Schmidt	Forward	K.U.	2
8:36	Gordon for	Wilkins	Guard	K.U.	
8:37	Hodges for	Belgard	Guard	K.U.	1
8:37	Klingman for	Fisher	Guard	Ames	$\frac{1}{4}$
8:38	Game ended.				

D. SUMMARY OF FOULS

	Insertion	Omission
1. Running with the ball	1891	
2. Hitting the ball with the fist	1891	
3. Holding the ball with other than hands	1891	1908
4. Moving basketball on rim	1891	
5. Shouldering an opponent (charging)	1891	
6. Holding an opponent	1891	
7. Pushing an opponent	1891	
8. Tripping an opponent	1891	
9. Striking an opponent	1891	
10. Kicking the ball	1893	
11. Delaying the game	1893	
12. Unnecessary roughness	1894	
13. Touching the ball before the center	1894	
14. Others than captain talking to officials	1894	
15. Entering the free throw lane	1895	
16. Carrying the ball out of bounds	1895	
17. Interfering with the free throw	1895	
18. Passing to another on the free throw	1896	
19. Double foul	1896	
20. Hacking *	1897	
21. Tackling *	1903	
22. Blocking	1905	
23. Making personal contact in scrimmage	1905	
24. Throwing for goal when the ball is dead	1905	
25. Throwing for goal after dribbling	1905	1908
26. Using profanity *	1906	
27. Carrying the ball in from out of bounds	1908	
28. Touching the ball when thrown in from out of bounds	1908	
29. Pushing the player throwing for goal	1908	
30. Taking more than three times out each half	1908	1912
31. Disqualifying on the fifth foul	1908	1910
32. A second dribble	1908	
33. Adding the "charge into" to other contacts	1909	
34. Coaching from the side lines	1910	
35. Disqualifying on four personal fouls	1910	
36. Substituting without reporting	1912	
37. Charging into player between the offender and the goal	1912	

* These rules are retained but are included under other rules.

D. SUMMARY OF FOULS—*Continued*

	Insertion	*Omission*
38. Taking more than ten seconds to throw goal......	1912	
39. Taking more than three times out in each game...	1912	
40. Leaving the court without permission...........	1913	
41. Placing the hand behind the back on a jump ball..	1915	
42. Being on the floor without permission...........	1915	
43. Violating the rule of jump ball (hands on back)...	1922	1925
44. Entering the game after leaving it twice.........	1924	
45. Changing a player's number during a game.......	1925	
46. Interfering in any way with the opponent on the jump ball.................................	1925	
47. Tapping the ball before it reaches the highest point	1925	
48. Leaving circle before the ball has been tapped....	1930	
49. Disposing of the ball in three seconds by the post pivot man.................................	1932	
50. Dividing the field into two courts..............	1932	
51. Compelling the offense to make attack in ten seconds.................................	1932	
52. Prohibiting passing the ball into back court more than once.	1932	

E. CLASSIFICATION OF ATTRIBUTES DEVELOPED BY ATHLETICS AND GAMES

MUSCULAR DEVELOPMENT
1. Endurance
2. Strength
3. Symmetry
4. Vigor
5. Vitality

SKILL
1. Agility
2. Alertness
3. Co-ordination
4. Muscular Control
5. Physical Judgment
6. Reflex Skill
7. Speed

MENTAL
1. Generalship
2. Generalization
3. Initiative
4. Memory
5. Observation

EMOTIONS
1. Ambition
2. Enthusiasm
3. Joy (Victory)
4. Loyalty
5. Remorse
6. Self-confidence
7. Self-respect

SOCIAL
1. Co-operation
2. Leadership
3. Observing Rules
4. Sportsmanship
5. Team Work

MORAL
1. Concentration
2. Courage
3. Determination
4. Perseverance
5. Perspective
6. Self-control
7. Self-sacrifice

F. DEFINITION OF ATTRIBUTES DEVELOPED BY OR USED IN ATHLETICS

1. ACCURACY: Precision in action.
2. AGGRESSIVENESS: Pushing through regardless of the feelings of others.
3. AGILITY: Power to move quickly from one point to another.
4. ALERTNESS: Readiness to respond to a stimulus.
5. CONCENTRATION: Cutting out extraneous things.
6. CO-OPERATION: Working with team mates without prepared lines.
7. CO-ORDINATION: A muscle or group assisting another muscle or group.
8. COURAGE: Go ahead at risk of personal injury.
9. DETERMINATION: Holding to an activity through difficulties.
10. ENDURANCE: Ability or power to continue the action of the motor mechanism.
11. ENTHUSIASM: Expression of great interest.
12. GENERALSHIP: Ability to analyze attack and prepare defense.
13. GENERALIZATION: Planning the future from the past.
14. INITIATIVE: Efficiently meeting new conditions.
15. JUDGMENT: Weighing values and making decisions.
16. LEADERSHIP: Ability to inspire others to follow.
17. LOYALTY: Readiness to sacrifice for an institution.
18. MUSCULAR CONTROL: Using right muscle at right time and to right extent.
19. MUSCULAR DEVELOPMENT: Anatomical enlargement of the muscular system.
20. OBEDIENCE: Following instructions.
21. PERSEVERANCE: Holding the subject in attention when tired out.
22. PHYSICAL JUDGMENT: Ability to estimate the force and direction of moving objects.
23. PLAYING THE GAME: Strenuous effort to win, while observing the rules.
24. SELF-CONFIDENCE: Consciousness of ability to do things.
25. SELF-CONTROL: Keeping the emotions under control.
26. SELF-RESPECT: Consciousness that one has done the right thing.
27. SELF-SACRIFICE: Working for results though others get the glory.
28. SKILL: A series of co-ordinations.
29. SPEED: Power to cover distance in a short time.
30. STRENGTH: Ability to overcome resistance.
31. SYMMETRY: Development of parts of the body in their proper proportions.
32. TEAM WORK: Following instructions in a prepared play.
33. VIGOR: Ability to drive the mechanism without breaking.
34. VITALITY: Power to build up usable tissue.

INDEX